T0304225

Object Management

Object Management

Data Management 91

9-10 April 1991
Walsall England

Edited by
Roger Tagg and June Mabon

Routledge
Taylor & Francis Group

LONDON AND NEW YORK

First published 1992 by Ashgate Publishing

Reissued 2018 by Routledge
2 Park Square, Milton Park, Abingdon, Oxon, OX14 4RN
711 Third Avenue, New York, NY 10017, USA

Routledge is an imprint of the Taylor & Francis Group, an informa business

Publisher's Note
The publisher has gone to great lengths to ensure the quality of this reprint but points out that some imperfections in the original copies may be apparent.

Disclaimer
The publisher has made every effort to trace copyright holders and welcomes correspondence from those they have been unable to contact.

A Library of Congress record exists under LC control number: 92005171

ISBN 13: 978-1-138-33934-7 (hbk)
ISBN 13: 978-0-429-44111-0 (ebk)

CONTENTS

OBJECT MANAGEMENT – THE APPLICATIONS

OBJECT MANAGEMENT – THE IMPLICATIONS

INTRODUCTION

This publication comprises chapters based on the papers selected for presentation at DM91 – OBJECT MANAGEMENT, the two day annual conference of the British Computer Society Data Management Specialist Group (formerly known as the BCS Database Specialist Group).

The first part sets the scene with chapters explaining the background to Object Technology, what has been achieved to date and how it may develop in the short and long term. The second part examines some of the OO products and assesses the essential characteristics of an OODBMS.

Part 3 looks at applications which use Object Technology; how successful are they? are there any lessons to be learned? The last part brings together the OO products and applications and assessed the implications for Data Management and Systems Development.

The Contributors and Their Chapters

ROGER TAGG examines 'The Object Oriented Approach and its Relevance to Data Management' and offers a definition of the Object Oriented Approach and identifying features, which, by common agreement, one can expect to find. His chapter explains why some of the buzzwords emerging in the OO press are somewhat clumsy combinations of well loved examples of database and data management vocabulary and the still incomplete Object vocabulary. Roger concludes by stating there is a need for a fundamental cultural change away from the traditional 'procedure-on-data' approach, if we are to complete the transition to Object Management.

CHRIS STONE'S chapter 'Object Technology: Making Applications Interoperable in a Distributed Environment', highlights the increasing rate of change in businesses as a major reason why information systems developers have to find an equivalent increase in the speed with which they can respond with new applications. Object Technology can provide application developers with reusability. This improves the speed of development and also opens up the way to savings in programmer productivity and product quality. Chris acknowledges that there is still a lot of work to be done to develop Object Technology and he is helping to establish the necessary rapport between organisations to make this development happen.

'Making Object Stick' by **JOHN DANIELS** and **STEVE COOK** gives the programmer's view of objects and discusses the requirement to create objects which continue to exist between program executions. They consider an "ultimate goal of object oriented software developers" is to create an object store where, among other things, objects which make up a program can exist after the termination of the program, and objects can be accessed by a language different from that used to define the object. The chapter describes the gulf which exists between this "ultimate goal" and the reality of current OO offerings.

ROY THEARLE contributes 'A Survey of Object Oriented Database Systems'. His chapter is a brief survey of six prominent systems and it gives details of the current state of development, system architecture and data models. The survey is based on a similar exercise carried out as part of the SERC funded "Zenith" project involving the Universities of Kent and Lancaster.

CARLOS MIGUENS has been closely associated with developments in databases over a number of years. His chapter, 'Towards An Object Oriented Database – A Relational View', examines the changes required by the relational database vendors to make their products object oriented and the difficulties they face. It addresses the question of why relational products should even be considered for this new type of system.

'The ONTOS Object Database' occupies a prominent position in the OO market place. **TIM ANDREWS** describes the design principle behind the product, how it was developed and how it operates. ONTOS offers opportunities for enhancing productivity of C++ developers as well as a distributed database environment suitable for developing complex, performance intensive applications.

For organisations which want to move into Object Technology, **ELIZABETH OXBORROW** offers a yardstick against which they can evaluate OODBMS products. In her chapter, 'What Should Go Into An OODBMS Product (and why there is no simple answer!)', Elizabeth spells out the difficulties of comparing current OO products. Her chapter contains advice for vendors on how they should develop their products, if they are to make them attractive to users who have wide ranging and sometimes conflicting data management requirements.

Part 3 looks at OO applications. **ROGER TAGG** provides 'A Review of the Suitability of Various Applications for an OO Approach'. He offers a 10 dimension framework which can be used to categorise applications.

KEITH SHORT deals with 'Object Oriented Technology in Information Engineering'. His chapter described work performed to enhance Information Engineering to deal with a wider class of systems, specifically those systems which utilise operational database systems to provide higher level management support. He shows how Object Oriented Technology can assist the development of these systems, and how the technology can integrate with IE technology.

One of the foremost areas of interest for Object Technology is in Geographical Information Systems (GIS). **BOB BARR**, in his chapter 'Object Oriented Methodologies and Geographical Information Systems – A Natural Partnership?', observes that the high level of interest has still to be matched by a corresponding high quality and quantity of practical products and implemented systems.

JAN MACIEJOWSKI and **C.Y. TAN**, offer a 'Case Study: Computer Aided Control System Design'. This sees Object Oriented DBMS (using OO in a loose sense), as being at the core of a CAD environment. The chapter describes such an environment which the authors developed and implemented and which used a large proportion of object oriented techniques.

A prime market for Object Technology is office systems. **CHRIS MARSHALL'S** chapter explains 'Objects in the Office – the benefits for Users of NewWave'. This is a PC environment offering a graphical user interface and advanced object technology. The development of the NewWave product has its origins in a US government sponsored study on how PCs can be used to improve productivity and profitability.

Hierarchical Object Oriented Design (HOOD) was developed by the European Space Agency as a design method for ADA. **PETER ROBINSON** provides an overview of HOOD. Although HOOD is primarily intended for software to be developed in Ada, the object orientation of the design phase in HOOD is now being extended to the programming phase.

MALCOLM FOWLES sees 'Object Reusability: The Making of Data Management'. This chapter (and the one following) looks at the importance of Object Technology for Data Management. Malcolm considers that object orientation is pushing back the limitations on the successful management of shared resources, and hence is the making of Data Management.

COLETTE ROLLAND'S chapter 'Object Database Design', takes as its starting point the statement that conventional conceptual models do not fit well with the promising object oriented database systems. Colette presents an object oriented conceptual model which combines the assets of the conventional semantic models with the advantages of the object oriented approach.

THE BACKGROUND TO
OBJECT TECHNOLOGY

THE OBJECT ORIENTED APPROACH AND ITS RELEVANCE TO DATA MANAGEMENT

Roger Tagg
Chairman BCS Data Management Specialist Group's Working Party on Object Oriented Data Management

1.1 Introduction

Almost every speaker on topics with "object oriented" in their titles has a slightly different definition of exactly what "object oriented" means. The Object Oriented Approach is defined here as:

An approach to analysis, design and construction of computer applications which models the target system as a set of cooperating, independent processes ("objects") which operate by passing messages to each other which invoke procedures defined within the "receiver" object.

This contrasts with what can be called the "Procedure-on-Data" approach as enshrined in languages like COBOL and further developed in traditional database approaches, where the target system is modelled as a set of *functions* (linked by hierarchical and dependency relationships) operating on an orthogonal set of *data* (also structurally linked).

For the Object Oriented (OO) approach, the following fairly well-accepted set of features is also assumed to be included:

- encapsulation, i.e. hiding of all procedure and data details belonging to an object from outside objects, except for the names of the procedures that can be invoked and their parameter sequences. This means that all procedure (and data) details must be "private" to some object – which may be a single occurrence or a class of similar objects. Data and procedures are not allowed to exist freely in the system. Some objects, however, may be specialised towards storing data (i.e. data occurrences and Add/Amend/Delete operations on them), whilst others may be more geared to algorithms (e.g. interest calculations and the look-up tables of data which drive them).

- composite objects, i.e. the ability to build up objects as assemblies of constituent objects (and ultimately of atomic objects like integers, strings for simple rules). This is in contrast to normalised relations in an RDBMS where all such structures must be flattened out.

- extensibility, i.e. allowing the logic of a system (e.g. procedures, rules, data structures and inter-object relationships) to be changed just as dynamically as the data values.

- inheritance, i.e. support for object class hierarchies in which procedures and data belonging to a more generalised object class (e.g. "employees") are also available to a more restricted class (e.g. "salaried employees").

- overloading, i.e. allowing generic naming of similar procedure calls, the details of which depend on the receiving object; e.g. ADD could apply to many "data-storage" type objects.

- overriding, i.e. allowing the normal inherited procedure to be designed as "based on" an existing one but with different behaviour.

This approach contrast with the "database-oriented" methods that characterise today's methodologies and CASE tools, where the procedure/data split is at the highest level. Recently, a whole topic of "Object Oriented Database" has emerged – but this is really a misnomer, since to be Object Oriented it should be a "Data *and Procedure*" Base.

Of course, "Data Management" in the sense used by this Specialist Group, is much more than "Database", hence the name change a few years ago. Two key additional topics now included are "Data Administration" and "Analysis and Design in a shared data environment".

Even in the first of these, there is a recent trend to rechristening the task "Architecture Administration", which includes the management of shared procedure details as well as of shared data descriptions. A further change, to the term "Object Administration" does not seem to have caught on as yet – but maybe some people will soon be advertising themselves as "Object Administrators"!

Object Oriented Design (OOD), with its related terms Object Oriented Analysis (OOA) and Object Modelling, are the main vehicles in a change from an analysis/design approach based on a "procedure acting on data" view of the world to an approach based on "active communicating system elements". While this latter view fits in well with an application controlling a physical process through sensors, robots – and even the odd human intermediary – the former is a tried and tested approach for the sort of office procedures handled by traditional "DP" systems. Some of today's OOD methods are geared to a particular target language (often ADA), and others to OOPLs in general. Others are "objectised" versions of "database-oriented" design methodologies – most of which are relatively new and untried.

In the area of Object Oriented database management systems (OODBMS), we are currently faced with two largely opposing schools, namely "persistent OOPLs" and "extended relational". The former represents extensions to languages like Smalltalk, C++, and Algol to cater for "persistent" data (i.e. databases), while the latter adds to the concepts of a normal relational DBMS data types of "procedure" and "rule" (things which crept into some of the pre-relational DBMS but were expunged by the relational fundamentalists).

What most suppliers of OODBMS have yet to really get to grips with is the fact that nobody nowadays goes out to buy "just a DBMS" for any serious usage. What sells Oracle, Ingres, etc. are the add-ons (query, report writing, layout design tools, generators, even full CASE tools) as much as the DBMS itself. So at present, many OODBMS mean a step backwards in functionality to "pre-4th generation" for prospective users.

For any new computer technique to be successful, it has to provide a platform on which users and their organisations can get the applications they require implemented quickly and correctly. At present this is going to be a slow business with the Object Oriented approach, because of the unsettled state of the constituent technologies of object management. Furthermore, it is an open question as to whether the existing development methodologies, on which so much training effort has been devoted, can be enhanced to support the OO approach, or whether designers and implementers will have to "go back to school again" to learn a totally different technique.

To sum up, the advent of the Object Oriented approach impacts a number of aspects of Data Management, and does not imply merely the advent of OODBMS. The change from a Procedure-on-Data approach really means that we should stop talking about "Object Oriented Data Management" and start saying "Object Management" instead. However, there must be doubt as to how quickly any such cultural change will come for most practitioners.

OBJECT TECHNOLOGY: MAKING APPLICATIONS INTEROPERABLE IN A DISTRIBUTED ENVIRONMENT

Christopher Stone
Object Management Group, U.S.A.

2.1 Introduction

The business world is changing. Companies were once regional, national or, at most, multinational. Nowadays, many of them operate globally to benefit from economies of scale and the ability to move operations into nations where they are more profitable. Where many companies utilise a centralised, top-down control structure, they are now becoming more decentralised. Because of physical, cultural or business differences product divisions are better able to carry out their individual missions if they have more autonomy from the parent company. The challenge is how to give this freedom without compromising the integrity of the organisation as a whole. Here is where networked IT-support is needed. Competition forces companies to develop increasingly customised products at standard prices. All these changes are disturbing enough, but the problem is compounded by the fact that the rate of change is increasing as well. Addressing these pressures places a tremendous strain on an organisation and its information systems, because the change in the business environment has profound implications for how we build them. And it is in the latter area that changes are necessary to meet the business needs.

The needed information systems must be able to handle more complex information that will have to be stored and represented in a way that is natural and intuitive to end-users. We should be able to manipulate and "see" things represented in our information systems just the way we naturally view and address them in the real-world. Systems must be more flexible and responsive. It must be easy for the business to modify both structure and content of the information on the fly, without disrupting the business operations that depend on it. Information about special cases must be stored without unnecessary duplication. Quality, encompassing not just absence of defects, but also a high degree of usability, must improve. Future systems must meet all of these requirements without trading off any of them to obtain the other.

Development approaches and system solutions have alleviated but not fully resolved the problems to meet the above requirements.

2.2 Where We are Today

Database Management Technology has succeeded in addressing some of the issues in cross-run/cross-system data storage and access, but the various models – hierarchical, network, relational – have not fully resolved the problem of structure, leaving us with the choice between either rigid systems that capture complex structures and provide easy access (hierarchical and to a certain extent network databases) and flexible systems allowing multiple views but more complicated access (relational systems). This is a manifestation of the trade-off mentioned earlier. Hierarchical and network models have built-in structures that are difficult to change; relational databases solve the rigidity problem by pulling all high-level structures out of the database. But these have to be laboriously put together by the application programmers, making access more complicated. As the information we need to store becomes more complex – charts, diagrams, maps, voice annotation – we need information management systems that are *richly structured, highly flexible, easier to understand and access*, implying a different database model.

Concepts like Modular and Structured Design/Programming have been useful in coping with problems connected with system size and complexity and the coordination of people. However, system building is still a major effort and its products remain difficult to change or adapt, in spite of CASE-tool support. When considering data and instructions together, the conclusion must be, that the data must be modularised, right along with the procedures (information hiding), to prevent violation of module independence. This conclusion is not limited to data within programs, but includes data across programs (i.e. databases) as well. The merger of data and procedures has the potential of breaking down the last barrier between databases and programs. With data embedded in procedures it will be possible to build applications directly into the database, changing its role from a passive information repository to an active processor of knowledge, eliminating redundant code. However, this will require a different paradigm (model) and supporting technology. Object Technology involves the paradigm and technology to help to bring this about.

2.3 An Analogy

Rather than plunging right into explaining it, we will start with an analogy; after all, one way to understand something hard is to look around and see if it has been done before. When it comes to building complex systems that are also highly flexible, responsive to changes in the environment, and robust in quality, nature uses a powerful paradigm.

All life is constructed around a single building block – the cell. All of the infinite variety around us is built out of one kind of stuff. Looking at it, ignoring all the variation and complexity, we can establish that a

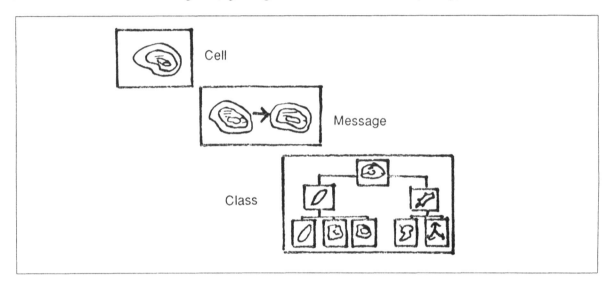

Figure 2.1: Cell hierarchy

cell is enclosed by a semi-permeable membrane that controls access to it. This *encapsulation protects its internals from outside intrusion*. The cell contains all the information (in its DNA) as well as the mechanisms for handling its behaviour. The second key principle is that cells interact through a *message based interface*. When a cell wants to affect the behaviour of other cells, it sends a chemical signal that triggers the desired response from those cells. The membranes filter incoming messages, only accepting the ones that are meaningful to the cell in question. The knowledge of HOW to react to the messages is situated within the receiving cell; the emitting cells "know" nothing about it. Communicating cells do not mess with each other's DNA, they stay out of each other's internal operations, minding their own business! The last key principle is, that the basic building blocks come in a wide variety of specialised forms and that they fall into neat hierarchical organisations in which each form shares the characteristics of all types above it in the hierarchy (Figure 2.1).

2.4 Object Technology

Object Technology is built on the very same principles (Figure 2.2).

• All software systems are built out of a single basic element – the object, which encapsulates the data

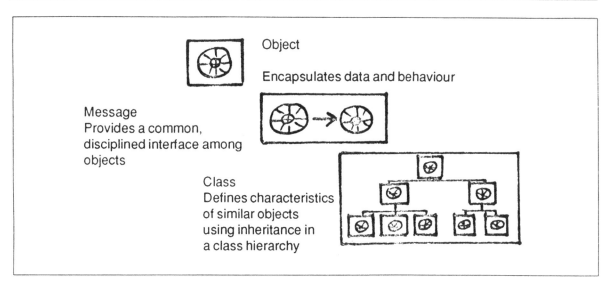

Figure 2.2: Object technology hierarchy

and procedures necessary for the creation of its behaviour(s) needed for its specific contribution to the environment. Access to the object's internals by other objects is impossible. It can only be triggered by activating one of its behavioural procedures.

- Objects interact through a message-based interface that allows them to cooperate without messing with the recipient object's internal processes or data. This scheme also protects the sending objects from having to keep track of the structure of any one object, leading to a more simple and loose communications pattern.

- Objects are grouped into a variety of types or classes, depending on their function, and these classes are arranged to fall into neat hierarchical organisations of, downwards increasing specialisation. Members in a hierarchy acquire the common characteristics from the associated higher levels.

Messages and encapsulation make the objects easier to modify. because only the object's own procedures can manipulate its internals, one can modify these procedures to effect the desired behavioural changes, or add new objects, without affecting the objects' environment (as long as the messages, that the added or modified object responds to, do not change). The same message call name can be used to activate different methods in different objects. This greatly simplifies complex systems because it reduces the number of different names programmers or users have to remember. There is no confusion because there is never a question about which method to carry out – it is the one that the object itself "knows about".

Living systems are organised into layers. Cells are organised into organs – like the heart and the brain. Organs are grouped into systems such as the circulatory system. Finally, these systems are tied together to form the organism as a whole. The most likely reason for such multi-level modularity is that it facilitates the process of *evolution*. The more independent organs and systems are, the more easily each of them can evolve into improved forms without disrupting the operation of the other organs and systems and the organism as a whole. And that is precisely why we should follow the same approach in building software.

A "class" in Object Technology is simply a template for a particular object. It contains the definitions of the procedures and variables that make up the associated objects because these are the parts that are the same for all objects or lower-level classes in the hierarchy (sub-classes). Many different classes can be defined to serve many different purposes. However, they are not defined in isolation, but rather as special cases of more generic classes (super-classes). This is analogous to the arrangement of living systems. This is an efficient arrangement because all the generic information is contained in one place, namely there where it is first needed, so that changes are localised. This mechanism stimulates reuse and productivity as well as standardisation and flexibility.

Also computer manufacturers designing a new machine do not start with a collection of diodes, resistors and transistors, and build a unique product. Rather they build up the machine in layers – chips, printed circuit boards, and the machine as an assembly of these boards – thereby using as many standard components as possible. We should be building software more like hardware, switching from building unique systems, starting every time from first principles, towards, as much as possible, assembling systems from generalised, reusable components. This offers far more reliable, adaptable functionality than designing or buying in monolithic systems that are difficult to adapt in their designed purpose (unless they have been designed and implemented in an Object Oriented way). It offers opportunities for internal development groups to compete with outside sources because of the possibility of increasing productivity and return on investment through reuse.

Object Technology can also be used to integrate existing systems by making use of its information and complexity hiding capabilities explained above. The operations and peculiarities of existing systems can be hidden behind a message-based interface by "enveloping" them in a "membrane", creating (pseudo) objects. Other systems integrated with it, become unaware of its internal operations, permitting it to evolve at its own pace without affecting its environment.

2.5 Conclusion

Although no panacea (learning curve, problems to be resolved in design and implementation methods, up-front investment and efforts to make reusability work), Object Technology offers interesting opportunities. To maximise the benefits of Object Technology, standards permitting the creation of multi-vendor, multi-platform object environment are necessary. The Object Management Group, an international consortium of more than 100 companies including Hewlett-Packard, Philips, Digital, Apple, SUN, AT&T, is working to resolve problems of distribution and interoperability to help achieve this goal.

MAKING OBJECTS STICK

John Daniels and Steve Cook
Object Designers Ltd

3.1 Introduction

As interest in the use of Object Oriented programming languages like C++ and Smalltalk grows, we must consider the wider implications. One of these is the effect of objects on the traditional relationship between program and data. The Object Oriented programmer wants a consistent view of the software terrain. In particular, he wants the objects he creates in his programs to have a life of their own; to continue to exist between program executions. For him, the problem is making objects stick.

3.2 The Object Oriented Programmer's View of Data

3.2.1 The Conceptual Architecture of Object Oriented Programs

One area of confusion facing new Object Oriented programmers is that the conceptual model of Object Oriented programs is significantly different from the implementation model, much more so than in traditional programs.

Figure 3.1 shows the conceptual view of an object, the one you generally meet in text books. Each object is an amalgam of data and the operations (functions or procedures) which access and manipulate that data. Think of it as a hard boiled egg. The yolk is the data held by the object. It is completely surrounded by the egg white, which represents the object's operations. The yolk's sole interface is with the white, unless you break open the egg – an action considered very bad form for objects. So although the object has data, the data are hidden and encapsulated. As far as other objects, or anything else for that matter, are concerned, the data don't exist. The existence of the data is merely implied by the existence of operations on them.

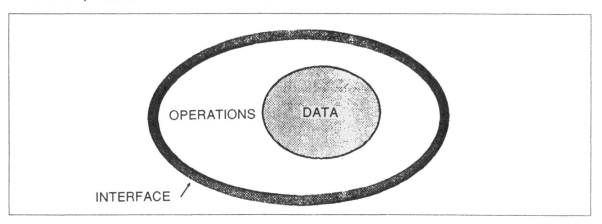

Figure 3.1: The boiled egg model of objects

Eggs have shells, too. We can consider the egg shell to be the defined interfaces of the object's operations. In just the same way that the data are hidden, so too are the implementations of the operations. It is the interface which is important to users of the object, not its implementation. We should be free to mix up the egg white – change the implementation – provided we keep the shell intact.

This view of objects as abstract data types gives the programmer considerable freedom of choice. He can delay decisions about the most suitable internal representation until long after the object's interface has been frozen. He can change that representation at any time without affecting other parts of the system. Indeed, Meyer[1] gives an example (pages 135-139) of an object representing a co-ordinate

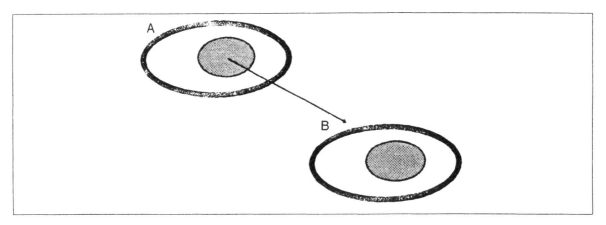

Figure 3.2: Object references

position which changes its internal representation from cartesian to polar and back again during execution!

In a truly Object Oriented program, all program behaviour is expressed only in terms of activation of object operations. The program "works" because the objects in it co-operate by activating each other's operations in response to external events. For this reason, the thread of control of an Object Oriented program is often hard to perceive.

An object A must have knowledge about the existence of object B in order to activate an operation of it. Therefore, assuming that the existence of object B is not registered in some global name space, object A must hold, as part of its state, a reference to object B (Figure 3.2). Thus the program consists of a set of interconnected objects, where the interconnections represent the unidirectional paths along which operation activations can be sent. The network is rooted at a point such that every object can be reached by traversal along the defined paths. This is shown in Figure 3.3. Any object which cannot be reached from the root cannot receive operation activations and is thus part of the program. Referring to Figure 3.3, imagine what would happen if object A decided to sever its link to object B. Object B can play no further part in the program. Logically, it no longer exists.

How are these inter-object references expressed? We assume that each object has a unique identity which remains fixed throughout the object's life. Each object is given its identity, by the program environment, when it is created. You must know an object's identity to activate one of its operations. These identities are held as state data to define inter-object relationships in the program network. It is important to note that these identities are completely separate from the state data held by an object. For example, the identity of a book object is not its title, nor even its ISBN. Titles are certainly not unique and whilst ISBNs are supposed to be, people do make mistakes! Furthermore, how many attributes of a book must change before it becomes a different book? Its title? Its ISBN? Its binding? Using system-allocated identities is the only sure way of avoiding problems. (For many examples of these ambiguities see the excellent book by William Kent.[2])

3.2.2 The Implementation Architecture of Object Oriented Programs

Let us now switch to a consideration of the realities of Object Oriented programming. It turns out that the implementation model of Object Oriented programs differs greatly from that described above. One reason for this is the redundancy of the conceptual view of objects. In most systems we find that we need many objects of the same kind. These objects are distinct, that is, they have different identities and different values for their state data, but they are identical in the structure of the data held and in both the definition and implementation of the operations they support. Clearly, we don't want to write the code for these operations many times, once for each object, nor do we want many copies of the code to exist.

So the implementation view of an object, however well disguised by the programming language or environment, is a simple data structure holding the data particular to that object. The structure contains

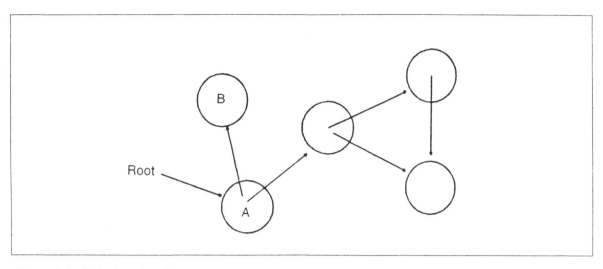

Figure 3.3: Object network

a definition of the kind of object it represents, thereby building a connection to the set of operations shared by all objects of that kind (Figure 3.4). The run-time system must use that connection to find the correct code to run whenever the object is asked to activate an operation.

Because of this factoring-out of the shared operations, writing an Object Oriented program does not consist of writing *objects*. Instead, the programmer writes *classes*. A class defines the shape of the data structure and the set of operations for one kind of object. Other features of Object Oriented programming, such as code sharing through inheritance, mean that there may be relationships between classes, but these have nothing to do with the relationships between objects which exist at run-time to form the logical program network. Indeed, reading class definitions is not an easy way of deducing that network.

All of the objects in the program network must reside in main memory, either real or virtual. Even virtual memory is a finite resource and so this memory must be managed. The memory occupied by the data structures of objects which can no longer be referenced must be recovered. This can be done automatically, as in Smalltalk, or with programmer assistance, as in C++. Since all the objects in which the program is interested reside in the same address space, the implementation of object identities is easy: they are nearly always simple memory addresses.

The Object Oriented programmer is not really interested in data at all. Such data as exist in his world are tightly encapsulated in objects. He is mostly interested in managing the creation and destruction of objects and data impinges on his world only when he must import them into his system to fill up objects or when he must export them for others to use.

3.3 The Database View of Data

3.3.1 The Program/Data Divide

Programs hold information and databases hold information. The information is called data in both cases. The similarity ends there. When a programmer wants data in his program to live longer than the execution of the program he must take special steps to copy the data from the program into another place: a persistent data repository, such as a disk file or, more grandly, a database. So, whilst a program and a repository may, during execution, contain the same data, those data are completely independent and, in some sense, "different".

The main memory of a computer is a dangerous place to be for important data. A power failure probably means their immediate demise. Databases usually go to great lengths to avoid data loss through machine failure and so programs often wish to commit important data to the database during execution.

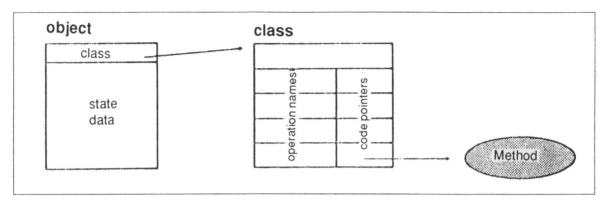

Figure 3.4: Object data structures

Another reason for storing data in a database is to allow them to be shared between programs. We may have a suite of different programs which all need to access the data or we may have several users all needing to access the data in the same way simultaneously. In either case we cannot lock-up the data in one program.

One big difference between programs and databases is that the program knows what the data mean but the database doesn't. To analyse or manipulate the data they must be brought into the program. (The word program is here used in the loosest sense, to include, for example, a SQL query.) Take the example of parts in a stock system. The retail price of the part and the cost price are related by the percentage markup. It may be a business rule that retail prices are always increased in line with cost prices. This knowledge will probably be captured in many programs but the data are held in a single shared database. All of these programs had better be sure they agree on what the data mean and how to manipulate them. Otherwise, the data will become inconsistent and useless. The meaning of the data, in any high-level sense, cannot be shared.

3.3.2 Structuring the Data

Databases normally define a number of simple data types, such as number, string and date. All data must, ultimately, be expressed in these types. The only unit of data structure in most databases is the record. A record is an ordered set of data, where each datum is of a simple type.

Inevitably, a program written in a modern language, and particularly one written in an Object Oriented Language, will hold its data in a much more complex structure than one-level records. The problems associated with mapping between records and such data structures have caused people to remark that there is an "impedance mismatch" between the two worlds of program and database. This problem is particularly acute with Object Oriented programs.

3.3.3 Queries, Triggers and Rules

The whole point of a database is that the data in it should have a long lifetime; longer than that of any program accessing it. Databases don't throw away data just because no program is looking at them or because they haven't been looked at recently. A record exists until its explicitly deleted. Although some databases arrange their records in a network, the modern trend is to allow more general access. A network database is similar to the Object Oriented program network described above; particular records are located by navigating along the fixed connections between them. A more general mechanism is to arrange all records of the same type into a table and retrieve particular records by formulating a query predicated on the values held by the records in particular fields. This is how relational databases operate. It is still possible to navigate through relational databases by following inter-records links (via unique keys) but they are not optimised for this.

A particular feature of relational databases is that records have no identity separate from their contents. Instead, a field or combination of fields of the record, called the unique key, are used to uniquely identify it. Since the value held in this field or fields may be held in other records as an inter-record reference (foreign key) it cannot be changed.

Recently, some relational database systems have begun to allow the definition of rules and triggers which are stored in the database. The purpose of these is to capture the most important semantics of the data, usually those associated with database consistency, and make them shared by all data users. In this way, databases are beginning to overcome some of the problems highlighted above, although, at present, rules and triggers tend to be severely limited in their capabilities.

3.4 The Goal: A Shared Persistent Object Store

The ultimate goal of Object Oriented software developers is to utilise a shared persistent object store. This store would be closely integrated with, but distinct from, programming environments. It would have the following characteristics.

- Objects which make up a program can exist after the termination of the program and until explicitly deleted. This persistence must be automatic and transparent.

- Particular objects can be located either by network traversal or query. During execution a program could extend its object network by identifying objects using queries. Once located, any network connections held by the object will automatically be traversed to locate other objects.

- Queries for object identification are expressed in terms of object interfaces and not the values of the data encapsulated in them. For example, a person object might have operations which answer both the age and date of birth of the person. We should be able to locate people objects by either criterion: "find all people born before 1st January 1960" or "find all people older than thirty years". It should not matter that the hidden implementation of people objects stores only their date of birth as state data and merely computes, on demand, their age.

- The persistent object must be complete. That is, both the data of the object and the implementation of its associated operations must reside in the database and, therefore, be shared.

- It must be possible for objects to be accessed by programs other than that which created them.

- Concurrent access and atomic transactions must be supported and controlled.

- The program which accesses the object can be written in a language different from that used to define the objects' behaviour and programs written in different languages can share the same objects.

Something interesting arises when we consider this specification. The object store described above holds a network of inter-connected objects which can communicate by invoking operations on other objects. Operations on stored objects always execute (logically) within the store, Each object has data and associated operations. This is exactly the conceptual architecture of an Object Oriented program! So, we should think of this store not as a database, but as a special kind of Object Oriented program which is resilient to power-loss and machine failure (well, as much as anything can be), which can receive object operation activations from outside its boundaries and which protects its objects against concurrent update. Our total system might comprise several such stores and other normal, non-resilient, programs.

3.5 Routes to the Goal

For the moment let us assume that the specification above represents the desired goal for persistent Object Oriented systems. Let us consider alternative routes by which we might reach that goal.

The problem to be faced is the gulf between the view of data represented by Object Oriented programming technology and that represented by current (mainly relational) databases. We suggest four alternative strategies that might, in different time-frames, bridge that gulf.

3.5.1 Do-It-Yourself

This route hardly represents a systematic route to achieving the goal. Here we suggest that the application programmer manually devises and codes a mapping between each kind of object in his program and an equivalent representation in a database. A simple mapping would be for the (relational) database to contain a table for each class of object which needs to be stored. Each object is stored in one row of the table. Inter-object references could be converted to the equivalent unique key or translated into some other private identity which is a stored attribute of each object.

Specific retrieval queries could be hard-boiled into routines associated with each class, providing a mechanism for creating and extending the program network. These queries might also be used to follow inter-object references. This system could not support arbitrary queries but then, in practice, they are rarely needed.

Although unsophisticated, the do-it-yourself technique can produce an efficient interface to a database, at the expense of much programmer effort. This technique represents the route followed by most OO programmers today. It is only a little more labour-intensive than the effort of accessing a database from C and does have some advantages over the techniques described below. In particular, it is probably the only one of the four which allows Object Oriented programs to take an Object Oriented view of existing databases, although, of course, there is nothing to stop Object Oriented programs accessing databases in just the same way as do conventional programs.

3.5.2 Build a Bridge

For this route we suggest the construction of a smart interface layer which transparently connects programs written in standard Object Oriented programming languages to standard relational (or other) databases (probably using standard SQL statements). This represents a direct attempt to build a bridge over the technology gulf. The layer would need a general algorithm for mapping from objects to tables and vice-versa. Retrieval queries could be automatically synthesized from program requests expressed in object terms.

This route requires the construction of something which looks a like a current Object Oriented database at the front-end and uses a current database manager as its back-end. Whilst we believe such a layer could be constructed and could support all Object Oriented concepts, the performance of the resulting system is likely to be poor.

There are no major products on sale which follow this route. The Iris system, a research project by Hewlett-Packard,[3] rumoured to become a product soon, is based on this principle.

In theory, the data held in the back-end database would be available to non-object-oriented programs as well. In practice, it may be that unnatural usage of the database features renders this impractical.

One problems with this route is that, whilst it promises close integration with the programming language, such integration really requires programming at the meta-object level if it is to be truly transparent. Thus it seems reasonable to attempt such integration with languages which support meta-level programming, like CLOS or Smalltalk, but less attractive with languages like C++. Practical experience of the authors with this route would seem to bear this out.

3.5.3 Extend the Language

A third possible route is to ignore current database technology and build a completely new data storage mechanism which efficiently maps the data of objects from backing-store to main memory and back again, keeping their inherent structure intact. It would be possible to construct this new database to fully support all Object Oriented programming language features in an efficient manner. The resulting database model would be reminiscent of network databases.

We call this route *Extend the language* because the programmer is not directly concerned with the databases at all; he sees extensions to his programming language which deal with the management of persistent objects.

A major advantage of this route is the performance potential it offers. Inter-object references can be translated into natural programming language identities, usually memory addresses as objects are brought into main memory. This reduces the overhead of following a reference to a memory de-reference. Since the object store understand such connections intimately, it can cluster connected objects and optimise their storage and retrieval.

This is the route being taken by the majority of Object Oriented database developers.

3.5.4 Mimic the Language

A fourth possible route is to extend the data-structuring and rule triggering capabilities of existing relational databases to mimic the Object Oriented concepts found in Object Oriented programming languages, This approach does not eliminate the technology gap but reduces its width. The objective is not to build a bridge but to render it unnecessary; ask programmers to make a short leap rather than provide a bridge.

One advantage of this route is the generality of the resulting database. The Object Oriented extensions exist but you do not have to use them. Also, these extensions would be built on many years of experience and refinement of existing technology, particularly in the area of query optimisation.

On the other hand, we feel unsure about the extent to which the gulf can be narrowed whilst remaining within the bounds of existing relational theory.

This is the route recommended by relational database vendors.

3.6 The State of the Art

3.6.1 The Issues

None of the routes described above address all the important issues surrounding the development of the shared persistent object store which is our goal. Indeed, they mostly ignore them. We can conclude, therefore, that if those routes really represent viable routes to the goal they represent only the first steps on a long path.

We believe that there are four essential points to be addressed:

* Queries must be expressed in terms of operation results not data values. This constraint make efficient indexing very difficult.

* The code for the operations must be in the database so that it can be shared.

* The database and access to its contents must be programming language independent but, conversely, closely integrated with programming language.

- We must standardise the object model, object query languages and programming languages interfaces. Only by such standardisation will we be able to approach the interchangability promised by relational databases and SQL.

3.6.2 Where are We?

Taking each of the four points listed above in turn, we can assess current products to see how well they are doing.

We know of no commercially available products which allow queries to be expressed in terms of operations rather than data values. This is particularly significant in the case of the Object Oriented database products, since it means that object encapsulation must be broken in order to specify queries. Although this can be masked to some extent by disciplined programming, we consider this a significant deficiency.

The only steps towards putting the code of objects in databases have been the provision of rules, triggers and user-defined functions in some relational databases and, to a lesser extent, in Object Oriented databases. We would seem to be a long way from achieving our ambition to store complete objects in databases.

Relational databases are language independent in the sense that you can embed SQL in most languages. However, no one would claim that they are closely integrated with programming languages. The situation with Object Oriented databases is even worse. Since the stored structure of an object is closely related to its program structure these databases currently insist that all programs which access objects of a particular class have identical class definitions and hierarchies. Furthermore, this makes it impossible or, at best, very tricky, to access stored objects created by one programming language from another.

Standardisation is in its very early stages. The Object Management Group, an association of many computer companies, is one body attempting to define a standard object model but much remains to be done. Several query languages have been proposed. OSQL, a language syntactically similar to SQL, is provided as part of the Iris system and is typical of work in this area. There is at present no standardisation between the program interfaces of the different Object Oriented databases, making the development of portable code impossible.

3.7 Conclusion

We believe that Object Oriented databases, such as those developed by Versant, Ontologic and Hewlett-Packard, represent the most promising step towards our defined goal.

However, these systems are concerned primarily with the efficient movement of object data between main memory and backing store. Whilst this is an essential foundation of a shared persistent object store, it is only a beginning. The route to achieving the shared persistent object store involves tackling the problems of sharing and connectivity, as well as storage. True object sharing is a long-term goal, requiring a standard for the interaction of objects in different address spaces. Even so, we feel that the next step for these systems must be to improve their support for object sharing, albeit in a limited way. At present, when several users of an Object Oriented database are all operating on the same persistent object each have a copy of its data. Whilst the transaction mechanism of the database prevents simultaneous update it does nothing to ensure that each user maintains an up-to-date copy. Cooperative working in a distributed environment requires this facility.

Persistent object stores are in their infancy. Despite this, current products can be of great value in certain application areas. We are judging them against an ideal and not against their usefulness. In particular, current Object Oriented databases offer efficient solutions to the problem of storing intricate data. However, for the humble Object Oriented programmer concerned only with making objects stick, there is a long way to go.

References

[1]   Meyer, B.: *Object Oriented Software Construction*, Prentice Hall, 1988.

[2]   Kent, W.: *Data and Reality*, North Holland, 1978.

[3]   Kim, W. and Lochovsky, F. (eds): *Object Oriented Concepts, Databases, and Applications*, Addison Wesley, 1989. See chapter ten.

OBJECT MANAGEMENT
The Products

A SURVEY OF OBJECT ORIENTED DATABASE SYSTEMS

R. W. Thearle
University of Kent at Canterbury

4.1 Introduction

There has recently been an increased amount of interest in the use of Object Oriented techniques in the database management field. Several database systems based (to a varying extent) on the Object Oriented paradigm have been designed and implemented. The aim of this chapter is to give a brief survey of some of the more prominent systems, including details of their status, architectures and data models.

The next two sections contain respectively information regarding the terminology used in this survey and the criteria used for comparing the systems covered. Section 4 lists the systems covered, including the reasons for their selection, and gives brief details of some other existing systems. The remaining sections each give details of a single Object Oriented database system.

This survey is based on a similar survey produced as part of the SERC-funded Zenith project involving the Universities of Kent and Lancaster.[1]

4.2 Note on Terminology

Interest in Object Oriented databases arose simultaneously in both the relational database and Object Oriented programming communities. In addition, input has also come from application areas such as software engineering and computer-aided design. One result of this is that different groups use terminology from different backgrounds, thus the same term may have different definitions for different people. Therefore, any survey of the field should include definitions of terms used.

The terminology used here is based on that given in R.W. Thearle, E.A. Oxborrow, 'Standardisation of Terminology in Object-Oriented Databases'.[2]

4.3 Criteria for System Comparison

Each system surveyed is described in terms of its status, its architecture, and its data model.

The status of a system covers its background, its stage of development and current availability, and the aims behind its production (e.g. commercial or research).

The architecture of a system covers design and implementation details, including:

- facilities provided, including embedded language and query interfaces;

- hardware and software details;

- capabilities, including performance and distribution.

The data model of a system covers the nature of the data stored in the system, and the degree of correspondence to the criteria for Object Orientedness given in 'The OODB System Manifesto: A Political Pamphlet'.[3]

4.4 Systems Covered

The following systems are described in detail in this survey:

EXODUS, Gemstone, Iris, ORION, O_2, PCTE/PCTE+.

These systems were selected mainly for their prominence, except for EXODUS, chosen because of its unusual architecture and PCTE/PCTE+ to provide comparison with systems with non-database backgrounds.

Two other systems which would have been covered but which are omitted to avoid duplication between chapters are ONTOS and Postgres. There are also a number of other systems and models in existence which deserve mention, but which will not be covered in detail; these include

- AIM-P, an IBM system from Heidelberg;

- Alltalk,[4] a system from Eastman Kodak providing persistent Smalltalk objects in Unix;

- Arjuna,[5] an Object Oriented programming system with persistent objects prototyped at the University of Newcastle;

- Aspect,[6] a Software engineering environment produced by ICL, Systems Designers, MARI and the Universities of Newcastle and York, which has been used (as PK) by British Aerospace;

- AVANCE,[7] a research prototype object management system from the University of Stockholm;

- Cactis (Colorado ACTIve Semantics),[8] a data model designed and implemented at the University of Colorado, aimed at efficient handling of highly complex derived information;

- Commandos, an ESPRIT funded project for designing an Object Oriented system;

- Damokles,[9] a database system supporting complex objects, implemented at FZI;

- ENCORE,[10] an experimental Object Oriented database for programming support, implemented at Brown University using the ObServer database;[11] recent work on ENCORE has concentrated on type evolution in an Object Oriented database;

- Genesis,[12] an extensible database management system based on the DAPLEX functional data model;

- IFO,[13] a data model designed at INRIA and the University of Southern California, for use in theoretical computer science research;

- JASMIN,[14] an Object Oriented database system from Fujitsu;

- KIWI, an Object Oriented database system developed by Philips in Eindhoven;

- ODM,[15] an Object Oriented data model designed at the University of Minnesota, with support from Honeywell, Sperry and Control Data;

- OZ+,[16] an Object Oriented database system designed for engineering office information systems, implemented at the University of Toronto on a network of Sun workstations;

- PS-Algol,[17] an Algol based Object Oriented programming language with persistence, developed by the Persistent Programming Research Group at the Universities of Glasgow and St. Andrews. It has been used to produce several prototype database systems;

- VISION,[18] a currently available Object Oriented database system developed at Innovative Systems Techniques especially for the commercial marketplace;

- XSQL, an IBM in-house Object Oriented database model;

- Zeitgeist,[19] a persistent object system being prototyped at Texas Instruments.

4.5 EXODUS

4.5.1 Status

EXODUS (EXtensible Object Oriented Database System)[20] is a skeleton Object Oriented database management system designed at the University of Wisconsin.[1] The main concept behind EXODUS is that there is currently no universally accepted Object Oriented database model, and therefore EXODUS should be sufficiently adaptable to support any emerging standard. The EXODUS system has been implemented, and configurations for supporting particular data models have been produced.

4.5.2 Architecture

The EXODUS system consists of two components present in all configurations (the storage object manager and the type manager), and two which are configured according to the data model being used (access methods and operator methods). Using these, a query optimiser and compiler, a query parser, and a DDL support tool are generated automatically.

The storage object manager is that part of the system which is responsible for low-level storage. It is designed to be independent of the data model used.

The type manager is responsible for maintaining the object class hierarchy, and keeping track of links between classes and instances.

The access methods and operator methods provide respectively a configurable interface to the storage object manager and user database manipulation operations.

4.5.3 Data Model

The data model of EXODUS is necessarily low-level; objects are effectively blocks of binary data. However, the type manager provides support for subtyping and abstraction of procedures.

A version of EXODUS configured to the specifically designed EXTRA data model has been produced. EXTRA is superficially the same as the Postgres model, but with a few additional features.

4.5.4 Summary

EXODUS is one of only three Object Oriented database management systems designed in this manner (the other two being Genesis and Zeitgeist). It is not yet known whether EXODUS is sufficiently versatile to handle complex Object Oriented models.

4.6 GemStone

4.6.1 Status

GemStone is an Object Oriented database management system designed and implemented at Servio Logic Corporation.[21] It uses a customised (persistent) version of the Smalltalk '80 language and runs on personal workstations, including Suns (3 or 4), Vax workstations, IBM-PCs, Tektronix machines and Macintoshes. The complete system is currently available commercially.

4.6.2 Architecture

GemStone uses a host/client architecture. The host machine, usually a Sun or Vax workstation, runs a database monitor, which is responsible for storage space allocation. Client machines run applications via GemStone sessions (which can be run either on the host or client) and communications software. The applications can access the GemStone session via C, Smalltalk '80, Smalltalk/V or Topaz[2] interfaces. Alternatively, the user may use the OPAL data definition and query language provided as part of the GemStone session.

4.6.3 Data Model

The GemStone data model is taken almost directly from Smalltalk '80. Objects are distributed amongst classes, as instances, with the information common to all objects in a class extracted and stored as the class's type definition. Access to objects is only permitted via messages to the object's procedural interface.

Gemstone classes are arranged in an inheritance hierarchy, where the upper levels of the hierarchy contain the available predefined object classes.[3]

4.6.4 Summary

GemStone is a good example of a system which fulfils all the requirements from 'The OODB System Manifesto (A Political Pamphlet)',[3] whilst being a comparatively mature system.

4.7 Iris

4.7.1 Status

Iris is an Object Oriented database management system based on a functional database model, designed and prototyped at Hewlett-Packard Laboratories.[22] It is included in this survey because the underlying data model supports high-level structural and behavioural abstractions.

4.7.2 Architecture

The central part of the Iris architecture is the Iris kernel, which implements the Iris data model, and provides a server for various client interfaces. Beneath the Iris kernel is the Iris storage manager, which is a conventional relational storage subsystem (HP-SQL), extended to allow the generation of object identifiers.

The Iris Kernel currently supports four interfaces – a graphical editor for manipulating metadata and function values, a C language interface, an interactive OSQL (object SQL) interface and an embedded OSQL interface.

4.7.3 Data Model

The Iris data model is purely functional in nature. The objects it supports are unusual in that they have no state; all values, relationships and behaviour are stored as functions.

Objects are divided into classes which share common functions, with a distinction being made between those objects which are directly representable (integers, strings, etc., literals) and those which are not (non-literals). Non-literals are organised into a type structure that supports subtyping.

Iris metadata is modelled in terms of the Iris data model.

4.7.4 Summary

The Iris system satisfies all the criteria for Object Orientedness given in 'The OODB System Manifesto (A Political Pamphlet)',[3] but has the drawback that it is implemented on top of a relational database system.

4.8 ORION

4.8.1 Status

ORION[23] is a series of Object Oriented database systems using the Smalltalk object model and designed and implemented at MCC.[4] The ORION systems have been implemented in Common LISP on a Symbolics 360 LISP machine, and ported to Sun workstations running Unix.

The systems in the series are:

ORION-1 – a single processor system;

ORION-1SX – a distributed client/server system;

ORION-2 – a fully distributed system.

4.8.2 Architecture

The architecture of the ORION-1 and ORION-1SX systems consists of four parts – a storage subsystem responsible for low level data access facilities; a transaction subsystem responsible for maintaining database integrity whilst allowing for multiple concurrent transactions; an object subsystem that provides high level data management facilities; and a message handler responsible for dealing with object invocation. The transaction and storage subsystems are divided between the server and the clients, the two halves being connected by a communication subsystem.

4.8.3 Data Model

The ORION data model is heavily based on that provided by the Smalltalk '80 programming language. It includes extensive data type evolution facilities.

4.8.4 Summary

The ORION systems are direct implementations of a persistent Smalltalk Object Oriented model, with varying degrees of distribution. ORION-2 is rare in that it is completely distributed; most Object Oriented databases rely on a client/server architecture.

4.9 O_2

4.9.1 Status

O_2 is an Object Oriented database system designed by the Altair consortium, funded by IN2 (Siemens), INRIA, and LRI (University of Paris).[24] A prototype system running on Sun workstations has been produced and distributed for evaluation, and work on a complete implementation has begun.

4.9.2 Architecture

O_2 uses a three-layered client server architecture. The three layers in the system are the schema manager (SM), the object manager (OM), and the disk manager (WiSS).[5] The storage manager is responsible for manipulating object classes and procedures; information regarding these schemas is stored in O_2 objects. The OM handles persistent and non-persistent complex objects. It is also responsible for handling communications between the application, which exists on the client, and the WiSS, which exists on the server. The WiSS is responsible for low level storage and concurrency control.

O_2 currently supports several interfaces, including:

* programming language interfaces for C and Basic (CO_2 and $BasicO_2$);

* a query language using an SQL-like syntax;

* an object user interface generator (LOOKS);

* a graphical Object Oriented programming environment (OOPE) implemented using CO_2 and LOOKS.

4.9.3 Data Model

The data model used in O_2 is a highly Object Oriented one, devised specifically to support the concepts of

* object identity;

* object classes and encapsulation;

* subtyping and inheritance;

* over-riding and late binding.

As was noted above, the O_2 metadata is modelled using the O_2 data model.

4.9.4 Summary

O_2 is a relatively recent system that is rapidly increasing in importance.

4.10 PCTE/PCTE+

4.10.1 Status

The original PCTE[6] system specification was written as part of the ESPRIT software engineering initiative with the intent that it would be used as a common basis for software engineering research in Europe.[25] Implementations of PCTE are currently available for Sun workstations (among others). The PCTE+ system is a later version of PCTE which corrects omissions in PCTE, mostly concerned with making PCTE suitable for use on high security military projects.[26] It is currently being implemented. Specifications of both PCTE and PCTE+ are available in either C or Ada.

4.10.2 Architecture

The GIE implementation of PCTE consists of three main parts – a central kernel, controlling access to the object store, a set of database manipulation and other tools, and a user interface agent for coordinating applications' access to the user interface facilities. The PCTE+ specification includes details of requirements for distribution, configuration management and security control.

4.10.3 Data Model

Despite being derived from software engineering databases, the PCTE(+) database is sufficiently Object Oriented for it to be included in this study. The PCTE object store consists of a collection of objects with inter-relationships (links), where objects and links are divided into classes. The classes form a strict hierarchy.

PCTE data definitions are stored in a collection of clusters, each of which contains the descriptions of a set of related classes, comprising a partial view of the complete database. These clusters are themselves database objects.

4.10.4 Summary

The main feature which prevents PCTE(+) from being Object Oriented is its lack of encapsulation; that is objects are merely collections of data which have no procedural information associated with them.

Notes

1. Despite the similarity of approach between this system and Genesis, and the related names, the two systems are not connected.
2. A command line interface.
3. There are arguably too many of these, since the class 'integer' is at the fourth level of the hierarchy.
4. Microelectronics and Computer Technology Corporation, Austin, Texas.
5. Wisconsin Storage System.
6. Basis for a Portable Common Tool Environment.

References

[1] R.W. Thearle, 'Survey of Object-Oriented Databases', *UKC internal report*, 1989.
[2] R.W. Thearle, E.A. Oxborrow, 'Standardisation of Terminology in Object-Oriented Databases', *UKC internal report*, 1989.
[3] M. Atkinson *et al*, 'The OODB System Manifesto (A Political Pamphlet)', in *Proceedings DOOD '89*, Kyoto, Japan, December 1989.
[4] F. Mellender *et al*, 'Optimizing Smalltalk Message Performance', in *Object-Oriented Concepts, Databases and Applications*, ed. W. Kim, F.H. Lochovsky, 1989.
[5] G.N. Dixon *et al*, 'The Treatment of Persistent Objects in Arjuna', *Computer Journal* Vol. 32, No. 4, 1989.
[6] P.N. Robinson, I. Wilkinson, *Initial Impressions of Perspective Kernel*, BAe internal report BAe-WIT-RP-GEN-SWE-0113, 1988; P. Hitchcock, 'A Database View of the PCTE and Aspect', in *Software Engineering Environments*, ed. P. Brereton, 1988.
[7] A. Bjornerstedt, S. Britts, 'AVANCE: An Object-Management System', working paper WP-124, SYSLAB, University of Stockholm, 1988.
[8] S.E. Hudson, R. King, 'Cactis: A Self-Adaptive, Concurrent Implementation of an Object-Oriented Database Management System', *ACM Transactions on Database Systems*, Vol. 14, No. 3, September 1989.
[9] K. Dittrich, 'The DAMOKLES Database System for Design Applications: its Past, its Present, and its Future', in *Software Engineering Systems Research and Practice*, ed. K. Bennett, 1989.
[10] M.F. Hornick, S.B. Zdonik, 'A Shared Segmented Memory System for an Object-Oriented Database', *ACM Transactions on Office Information Systems*, Vol. 5, No. 1, January 1987; A.H. Skarra, S.B. Zdonik, 'Type Evolution in an Object-Oriented Database', in *Object-Oriented Concepts, Databases and Applications*, ed. W. Kim, F.H. Lochovsky, 1989.

[11]   A.H. Skarra *et al*, 'An object server for an Object-Oriented Database', in *Proceedings of International Workshop on Object-Oriented Database Systems*, 1986.

[12]   D.S. Batory *et al*, 'Implementation Concepts for an Extensible Data Model and Data Language', in *ACM Transactions on Database Systems*, Vol. 13, No. 3, September 1988.

[13]   M. Worboys *et al*, *The IFO Object-Oriented Data Model,* presented at Managing Geographical Information Systems and Databases, University of Lancaster, September 1989; S. Abiteboul, R. Hull, 'IFO: A Formal Semantic Database Model', *ACM Transactions on Database Systems*, Vol. 12, No. 4, December 1987

[14]   A. Makinouchi, H. Ishikawa, 'The Model and Architecture of the Object-Oriented Database System JASMIN', Working Paper, Fujitsu Ltd., Kawasaki, Japan, 1988.

[15]   M.A. Ketabchi *et al*, 'ODM: An Object-Oriented Data Model for Design Databases', in *Proceedings of ACM Annual Computer Science Conference*, 1986.

[16]   S.P. Weiser, F.H. Lochovsky, 'OZ+: An Object-Oriented Database System', in *Object-Oriented Concepts, Databases and Applications*, ed. W. Kim and F.H. Lochovsky, 1989.

[17]   R.L Cooper, M.P. Atkinson, 'Requirements Modelling in a Persistent Object Store/Type Hierarchies and Type Evolution using Deferred Binding Database Application Programs', *Persistent Programming Research Report 54*, Universities of Glasgow and St. Andrews, 1987.

[18]   M. Caruso, E. Sciore, 'The Vision Object-Oriented Database Management System', in *Advances in Database Programming Languages*, ed. F. Bancilhon, P. Buneman, 1990.

[19]   C. Thompson *et al*, 'Open Architecture for Object-Oriented Database Systems', *TI Information Technologies Laboratory technical report* 89-12-01, 1989.

[20]   M.J. Carey *et al*, 'Storage Management for Objects in EXODUS', in *Object-Oriented Concepts, Databases and Applications*, ed. W. Kim, F.H. Lochovsky, 1989.

[21]   *Gemstone Product Overview*, available from ServioLogic; R. Bretl *et al*, 'The GemStone Data Management System', in *Object-Oriented Concepts, Databases and Applications*, ed. W. Kim, F.H. Lochovsky, 1989.

[22]   K. Wilkinson *et al*, 'The Iris Architecture and Implementation', *IEEE Transactions on Knowledge and Data Engineering*, Vol. 2, No. 1, March 1990; D.H. Fishman *et al*, 'Overview of the Iris DBMS', in *Object-Oriented Concepts, Databases and Applications*, ed. W. Kim, F.H. Lochovsky, 1989.

[23]   W. Kim *et al*, 'Features of the ORION Object-Oriented Database System', in Object-Oriented Concepts, Databases and Applications, ed. W. Kim, F.H. Lochovsky, 1989; W. Kim *et al*, 'Architecture of the ORION Next Generation Database System', *IEEE Transactions on Knowledge and Data Engineering*, Vol. 2, No. 1, 1990.

[24]   O. Deux *et al*, 'The Story of O_2', *IEEE transactions on Knowledge and Data Engineering*, Vol. 2, No. 1, March 1990; C. Lecluse, P. Richard, F. Velez, 'O_2, an Object-Oriented Data Model', in *Advances in Database Programming Languages*, ed. F. Bancilhon, P. Buneman, 1990; F. Velez, G. Bernard, V. Darnis, 'The O_2 Object Manager: an Overview', in *Proceedings 15th International Conference on Very Large Databases*, 1989.

[25]   *PCTE: A Basis for a Portable Common Tool Environment, Functional Specifications*, 4th edition, available from Bull SA, 1986.

[26]   *PCTE+ C Functional Specification*, Issue 3, available from Yard Ltd., 1988.

The following general sources of information were also used:

A. Brown, *Object-Oriented Databases: Applications in Software Engineering*, 1991.

W. Kim, 'Object-Oriented Databases: Definition and Research Directions', *IEEE Transactions on Knowledge and Data Engineering*, Vol. 2, No. 3, Sept. 1990.

S.B. Zdonik, D. Maier, *Readings in Object-Oriented Databases*, 1990.

M.S. Jackson, 'Tutorial on Object-Oriented Databases', in *Information and Software Technology*, Vol. 33, No. 1, January/February 1991.

TOWARDS AN OBJECT ORIENTED DATABASE – A RELATIONAL VIEW

Carlos Miguens
Perfect Recall Ltd

5.1 Introduction

Relational Database Management Systems have had tremendous success in addressing many of the problems faced by DP managers and end-users, but in today's information hungry environments traditional technologies may not be enough.

Relational databases were originally designed to handle primitive data types such as characters and numbers, but in many applications and industry areas it has become clear that such an approach is not adequate. The inability of relation databases to easily handle and *understand* unconventional data (such as co-ordinates, arrays, matrices, vectors, fractions, etc.) and also deal adequately with business rules and procedures, has detracted from the initial productivity and ease-of-use gains offered by the technology.

In many cases, it has proved impossible or very difficult to reduce applications data to a simple form which can be easily represented in a relational database. Programmers and users have thus had to adapt their databases to incorporate complex information and business rules, which often meant coding of additional routines into each individual client application, adapting the system to the real world rather than the other way around.

With Object technology different types of business problems need to be addressed in different ways, creating a functional split within the database so that it deals with data, objects and knowledge. Clearly working in this fashion brings benefits and drawbacks, it has to be appreciated how the relational model concepts of tables, tuples and attributes map to the Object Oriented concepts of classes objects, slots and how inheritance could potentially be implemented.

The Object Oriented paradigm brings with it a new way of working and thinking to extended relational systems, or so called third generation systems.

THE ONTOS OBJECT DATABASE

Tim Andrews
Ontologic, Boston, U.S.A.

6.1 Introduction

The use of object databases is undergoing rapid growth in application development involving highly complex data models with strict performance requirements. Such application areas include CAD, CASE, GIS, and CIM. The ONTOS object database is in use in these and other areas. It provides an integrated C++ environment for highly productive application development, as well as state of the art graphical tools for interactive access with the object database and for the creation of graphical interface applications. ONTOS also contains unique features such as a complete set of meta classes, and integrated object SQL, and extensible storage management.

6.2 The ONTOS Usage Model

The ONTOS product is designed to be very easy to use by the C++ programmer. As an OODBMS, schema definition, object manipulation, and application implementation are all done in the same language. For ONTOS, the first language is C++; the industry accepted Object Oriented extension of C. Typically, once the application has been designed and the basic class structure identified, the developer creates C++ class definitions, which are passed to the ONTOS Classify utility which automatically generates the database schema in the ONTOS database. The interactive DBDesigner tool can also be used for this purpose, as described later.

Object Oriented application development, unlike traditional application development, separates the coding into two distinct areas: class implementation and application development. Class implementation develops the functionality designed and described by the class definitions which constitute the object database schema. Application development uses these classes to build the required customer functionality. In the ONTOS environment, all this work is done in C++ using any of a number of standard compilers on a variety of hardware platforms.

Before an application can be run, an object database must be registered with the ONTOS system. This is done using the interactive DBATool which leads the developer through a series of simple steps. With an object database registered and the application built, the process of testing, debugging, tuning etc, can proceed using standard techniques for C++ development. Thus ONTOS provides a highly integrated and productive environment for the C++ application developer.

6.3 The Interactive Tools

To further ease development and leverage efforts, ONTOS is adding interactive development capabilities. Currently available is the DBDesigner interactive graphical tool. DBDesigner is a window based tool built on the X Window system to run in standard environments such as Motif. It provides the ability to examine and modify both class definitions and object instances. Using DBDesigner, the developer can interactively create the object database schema rather than writing C++ class definitions using a standard text editor. DBDesigner then automatically generates the C++ class definitions into text files for use in implementing the classes and the applications, easing the development process.

DBDesigner can also be used to browse existing schemas and modify existing class definitions. At the instance level, DBDesigner displays instances of browsing and allows simple traversal of references between instances with mouse clicking. This makes it easy to interactively examine object structures and relationships in the object database. At any point the user can also modify the instances, making

DBDesigner an editor as well as a browser. This is very useful for correcting errors in the object database during development without having to write and compile a program, increasing programmer productivity tremendously.

ONTOS Studio, currently in early customer testing, is an interactive application development system, providing a high level graphical interface for creating window based applications. The developer simply "draws" the desired interface in the Studio environment, and the application is complete, creating a very powerful WYDIWYG (what you draw is what you get) system for developing interfaces to ONTOS applications. The burden of understanding complex window libraries and specifying detailed arguments including location on the screen to hundreds of calls is replaced by a direct visual interface in which the developer simply places windows in the desired location on the screen.

Support is provided for all standard window objects (called widgets) including windows, menus, buttons, scroll bars, bitmaps, editable text fields and more. All this is hooked directly to the ONTOS object database, and includes default layouts for any class in an ONTOS object database schema and the ability to interactively test an interface against actual objects in the object database. Studio also provides the ability to use customised routines written in C++ where the interactive mechanisms do not suffice. Studio thus provides state of the art capabilities to dramatically increase the quality of user interfaces while substantially decreasing both the effort and knowledge required to create them.

When combined, Studio with DBDesigner represent the next wave in object database development environments, where virtually an entire system can be developed without writing a single line of C++ code. Further, at any time C++ code can be added to fulfil any specialised requirements not met by these tools, retaining the high productivity and performance of the ONTOS base system.

6.4 The ONTOS Application Programming Interface (API)

The C++ application developer sees the ONTOS system mostly as a C++ class library. This makes it a natural interface for the C++ developer. The class library provides a great deal of useful functionality for the developer, masking most of the details of the object data management task and allowing the programmer to concentrate on the mechanics of the application. The ONTOS interface can be broadly divided into functional areas as follows: session control, transaction control, aggregate classes, meta model classes, exception processing, storage manager classes, and Object SQL classes. A few of these will be described.

6.5 Aggregate Classes

The ONTOS base system includes several container, or aggregate, classes which can be used by the C++ developer as building blocks for applications. These classes include dictionaries, arrays, lists and sets. The aggregate classes are all integrated into the object database and tuned for performance using disk access techniques such as extensible hashing and B*trees. Most applications make heavy use of these classes to create the necessary data structures to manage groups of objects. Having them available as a part of the base system eases application development significantly and increases performance due to the highly tuned implementations of these classes. This is a "classic" example of the benefits of reuse which accrue from Object Oriented development techniques.

6.6 Meta Schema Classes

A unique feature of the ONTOS system is that it is completely self descriptive: all the classes that comprise the schema are stored in the database as objects themselves, available to the programmer through a set of classes called "meta classes". The programmer sees them exactly as any other objects in the system, providing a uniform interface to all levels of the system. The availability of the meta classes makes possible many powerful capabilities. Perhaps the most valuable of these is that tools become standard applications. That is ONTOS Studio and DBDesigner are just standard applications written using the meta classes. This means that customers can take advantage of these tools within their own environment, and can also develop their own tools very easily. It also makes it possible to write interpretive environments which is not usually possible with C++. For example, ONTOS allows the execution of any C++ function from within an Object SQL query; this would not be possible without the meta classes.

6.7 Storage Managers

Another unique feature of ONTOS is the notion of storage manager classes. Object databases are generally required to deal with very different data structures from the very small to the very large. This is difficult to manage if only one interface to the disk storage management is used. This is the principle problem with previous generations of DBMS technology such as relational databases. The use of a single storage mechanism meant that high performance could only be achieved for certain data requirements.

Storage managers provide a mechanism to allow the use of any number of interfaces to the disk by providing a protocol for storage management in the Storage Manager class. Sub-classes using any techniques are permissible providing they adhere to the defined protocol. ONTOS provides two such classes today: a default storage manager suitable for highly concurrent applications with varying object sizes. Also provided is a group storage manager optimised for large numbers of instances with very small amounts of data. This requirement is typical of ECAD, MCAD, GIS and other application areas. Customers may also develop their own storage manager should new needs arise. This level of flexibility and extensibility is unique among database implementations and allows the integration of widely varying data structure requirements without sacrificing performance.

6.8 The Distribution Model

The ONTOS object database runs in a client/server environment and also provides true distribution for both process and data. Client and server processes can run on the same or different machines. A client process can be connected to multiple server processes which provide a distributed atomic commit using a two-phase commit protocol. Each server handles a separate data area providing data distribution and process distribution.

All of this object location mechanics is transparent to the application developer. This is due to the use of the ONTOS Logical Database. A logical database is a simple string name created by the customer. All applications use this name to connect to the database. The interactive DBATool creates the mapping between the logical database and the physical areas and host servers, isolating the application from this aspect of the system. Thus programs see all objects the same no matter where they are physically located. This also allows objects and data areas and host servers to be moved arbitrarily without affecting application programs.

6.9 Application Using ONTOS

ONTOS is currently in heavy use throughout the world in a wide variety of applications being developed for production environments. A representative sample is provided to provide some concrete examples of the use of the ONTOS system.

6.10 Manufacturing Planning

The ONTOS system is currently being used by a multibillion dollar manufacturing firm to plan freight shipment on its tens of thousands of trucks throughout the world. This is an extremely complex application involving route planning of the vehicles, knowledge of the weight of each vehicle at each point of delivery, and optimisation of the route planning to keep the vehicles filled and deliver goods to inventory sites in a timely fashion. There are some twenty to thirty programmers using ONTOS daily to develop this system for delivery.

6.11 GIS

GIS, or Geographical Information Systems, are used to provide electronic mapping functionality. Currently several ONTOS customers are developing GIS applications. The largest development effort is centred around a mapping system for county planning activities, where some twenty programmers have been working for over a year to develop an interactive environment for county planners. Another effort is taking place in Australia along similar lines.

6.12 ECAD

ONTOS is used at a multibillion dollar company for use in its next generation printed circuit board design system. This system provides simulation and layout capabilities for printed circuit boards, and is expected to be used by three to five hundred people once deployed.

6.13 Summary

ONTOS is a state of the art object data management system with a robust development environment for C++ developers, and an expanding graphical environment to further increase productivity of the developer. It provides a completely distributed database with unique characteristics for the development of highly complex, performance intensive applications, and is in wide use in commercial applications development today.

WHAT SHOULD GO INTO AN OODBMS PRODUCT (AND WHY THERE IS NO SIMPLE ANSWER!)

Elizabeth Oxborrow
University of Kent at Canterbury

7.1 Introduction

If you ask anyone who knows a little about databases what should go into a database management system (DBMS) product, they will most likely specify the facilities provided by current network or relational DBMSs. If you ask anyone who knows a little about Object Oriented databases what should go into an Object Oriented database management system (OODBMS) product, there will be a wide range of responses, not all of which will be consistent with each other. When purchasing a DBMS, one knows what to look for as far as user interface, software architecture and functionality are concerned. In the case of an OODBMS, though, there are currently so many variables that comparison between systems is very difficult. This problem will need to be resolved before OODBMSs take off as commercial products.

This paper takes a look at the problem. It provides an introduction to the important features of an OODBMS, and aims to provide a yardstick against which to evaluate OODBMS products.

7.2 Why Are OODBMSs So Different in Their Design?

Before answering the question: "Why are OODBMSs so different in their design?", it will be worth reviewing the DBMS situation. DBMSs were designed to satisfy the fairly well-defined requirements of the business data processing community in the 1970s. They started life as systems for the fast and efficient management of large volumes of inter-related record-based data, were then developed during the late 1970s to support facilities for ad-hoc queries, and were further developed during the 1980s to provide sophisticated interfaces for non-specialist end-users. All major systems now provide a query language (commonly SQL), a data manipulation language which may be hosted with a precompiler or compiled procedures (as with Embedded SQL) or self-contained (as in dBaseIV), and a forms-based interface. They are generally monolithic, "all or nothing" systems in the sense that one purchases a fully functional DBMS (although not necessarily all the user interfaces).

Such systems have, until recently, quite adequately satisfied the needs of those who use them. However, the requirements of the business data processing community have expanded in recent years; life has become increasingly complex, and users are demanding facilities for building databases which represent more realistic, less simplistic, abstractions of the real world. Enhancements to existing technology (e.g. enhanced relational systems such as Postgres[1]) are aimed at enabling this demand to be satisfied, but some database specialists have been asking the question: "Can the technology of the 1970s really support the data management requirements of the 1990s?"

From the relatively narrow viewpoint of business data management, one could give a fairly positive answer to the question just posed, although some of the more sophisticated requirements will inevitably be indirectly and not very "naturally" supported by this technology. However, if a broader view of data management is taken, the answer must be negative. There are now many non-traditional data management applications in a variety of different environments (e.g. computer aided design (CAD), office information systems (OISs), geographic and spatial information systems (GISs), project support (IPSEs), document processing), where the data to be managed is quite different in its structure and behaviour from the type of data for which DBMSs were designed, and where the concepts underlying the traditional DBMSs are found to be too limited. Thus, database specialists are now looking to new technologies for data management in the 1990s and beyond, and the one which has probably received the most attention recently is Object Oriented technology.

Some OODBMSs, especially those designed in the early days of OODB technology, have been oriented towards specific environments and applications, and hence, they often support different object models and functionality. In fact, the term: OODBMS, is ambiguous and has many interpretations. In some cases, it is applied to a DBMS which supports traditional database environments but is based on Object Oriented concepts. In other cases, it is applied to any system based on Object Oriented concepts providing persistent data management facilities (which are not necessarily suitable for traditional database environments). Furthermore, most traditional DBMSs are based on a standard data model (e.g. network, relational), but although each OODBMS is based on an object model, there is no equivalent standard, and the object models of various OODBMSs are sometimes quite different from each other. With many and varied environments and applications requiring sophisticated data management facilities, it is no wonder that there are so many different designs and that there is no simple answer to the question: "What should go into an OODBMS product?"

7.3 The Fundamental Features of an OODBMS – How Much of a Consensus is There?

An OODBMS must obviously contain database facilities, but it must also support Object Oriented concepts. The database system must provide for the end-user:

* persistence

* a query facility

together with important underlying data management facilities:

* secondary storage management

* concurrency

* recovery

To these DBMS features, the Manifesto of Atkinson *et al* adds eight mandatory Object Oriented features,[2] of which five can be identified as being fundamental;[3] these are:

* unique object identity

* types/classes

* inheritance

* complex/composite objects

* encapsulation

These Object Oriented features are illustrated in Figure 7.1 which shows an object uniquely identified as x, possessing characteristics appropriate to objects classified as sales-persons. Sales-persons have a commission, but they are also employees and as such they "inherit" the characteristics relevant to employees, including the components: name, job, address, age, and set of children. Object x is composite since some of its components are objects in their own right. Finally, the behaviour of object x, as well as its structure, is encapsulated within it, and other objects can only access x via the interfaces to its methods (indicated by the arrows in Figure 7.1).

The five Object Oriented features above have been widely discussed in the literature on Object Oriented systems as well as OODBMSs, and it is worth noting that they are now considered essential by the database community in general, not just by those interested in the Object Oriented approach. In Stonebraker,[4] amongst the propositions for new third-generation DBMSs, the first three cover: a rich type system with recursive composition, inheritance, and functions and encapsulation, while the fourth proposes unique system-defined identifiers when no user-defined ones are available (although this is a weaker proposition than the corresponding Object Oriented unique identity concept).

The remaining three mandatory features in the Manifesto are:

• overloading/overriding/late binding

• computational completeness

• extensibility of the type system

The first is important for effective support of inheritance and encapsulation, the second is essential for the implementation of methods encapsulated in objects and is complementary to the database query facility, and the third strengthens the type/class feature.

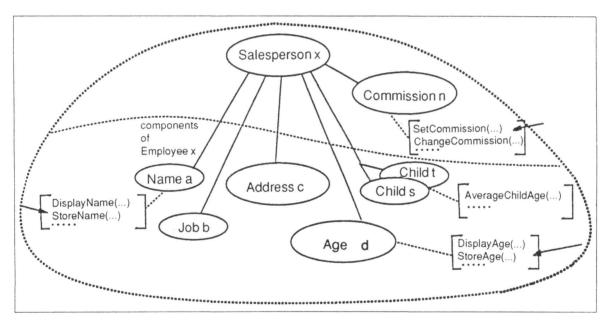

Figure 7.1: A Sales-person Object showing its immediate components and some of its methods and interfaces

A system containing all the features mentioned above might be assumed to provide an adequate OODBMS. Such a system would provide standard DBMS facilities with enhanced semantics, behavioural support and an object-based data model, but this would not go far towards satisfying future traditional and current non-traditional data management requirements. Future systems should enable multimedia and distributed facilities to be exploited and must provide adequate support for all the complexities and characteristics of various specialised environments. Additional non-standard options for secondary storage management, concurrency and recovery are required, and the Object Oriented features need to be enhanced. These are considered in section 7.4.

A further additional feature is system extensibility/reusability. A complete system capable of supporting all known data management requirements must inevitably either be an enormous monolithic system or be based on some reusable software which provides mechanisms for extension and/or selection of facilities for particular environments/applications. Over the last few years, much emphasis has been placed on extensibility and reusability, the objective being to provide generalised systems which can be tailored to particular environments. This will be considered in section 7.5.

7.4 Enhancing the Functionality of an OODBMS

The features introduced in section 7.3 are the result of applying the Object Oriented paradigm to traditional data management. The additional features discussed in this section are amongst those which were identified as a result of research being carried out on the SERC-funded Zenith project at the Universities of Kent and Lancaster. The first phase of this research involved an analysis of the data management requirements of IPSEs, OISs and GISs, as well as DBMSs.[5] This section introduces the following additional features/enhancements for an OODBMS:

* object relationships

* object groupings/collections

* object versions

* transparent multimedia and distributed facilities

* additional access control options

* additional concurrency options

* new secondary storage mechanisms

It should be noted that some of these are now appearing in current research prototypes and developed systems.

To illustrate some of these additional features, an example is provided in Figure 7.2. It represents a meeting known as x, which is a composite object containing a date, agenda, report and presentation. The agenda, report and presentation are themselves composite, with the presentation shown as having a title, abstract, duration and two video scenes. Below the horizontal line, the physical storage of some of these objects is illustrated.

7.4.1 Object Relationships

The composite object feature mentioned in section 7.3 provides support for the meeting object in Figure 7.2 together with all of its components (the objects enclosed within the dotted area), but not for the relationships between the meeting and the room it is located in and between the presentation and the person presenting it. Explicit support for such general relationships has been ignored until fairly recently. On the one hand, this is not surprising, since it is the complex internal structure and behaviour of objects (generally modelled via inheritance and object composition) which are of prime importance in the Object Oriented programming languages (OOPLs) from which OODB technology has evolved. But on the other hand this is surprising, since relationships have for some time featured in semantic data models and are an important element in data modelling in traditional databases. However, now that OODB research is starting to mature, the scope of the Object Oriented paradigm as applied to databases is being extended.

Effective support for relationships depends on the ability to define the full semantics and on the provision of system-defined functions for managing and accessing objects via these relationships. There are two main approaches to supporting relationships. They may be represented as first-class objects (e.g. in 'Semantic-rich User-defined Relationship as a Main Constructor in Object Oriented Database')[6] or as a special type of object characteristic distinct from attributes (e.g. Cactis).[7]

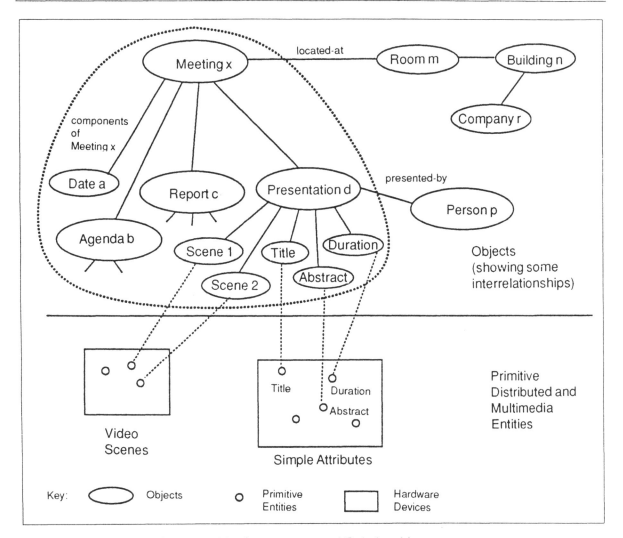

Figure 7.2: A Meeting Object and its Components and Relationships

7.4.2 Object Groupings/Collections

It is recognised that the new generation of DBMSs must subsume existing DBMSs if they are to be commercially viable.[4] Hence, the concept of an n-ary relation must be supportable, and system-defined functions which can be used to manipulate relations are required. In addition, more general object groupings or collections require support in other environments, for example, an in-tray in an OIS (Figure 7.3) or a software configuration in an IPSE (Figure 7.4). System support for sets, lists and bags provides a good basis for representing different kinds of grouping or collection.

7.4.3 Object Versions

In traditional database applications, objects are considered to be mutable; an object is updated by overwriting its previous state. However, this is done primarily for efficiency reasons,[8] and in many applications, traditional as well as non-traditional, the evolution of an object over time is important; in fact, in some it is essential. Hence an OODBMS must be able to support different versions of an object (and the history of those versions). In the example in Figure 7.2, the agenda and report may need to be versioned. As further examples, a software company must maintain information about different versions of their products, while in engineering, the evolution of a design may be very complex and the ability to revert to a previous design is important. Versions may be derived from a previous version in a linear fashion, but complex derivation trees (which may include variants of versions) are also possible. This is illustrated in Figure 7.5, which shows a single software module represented by a number of different versions and variants, with a version manager maintaining the version tree for the software module.

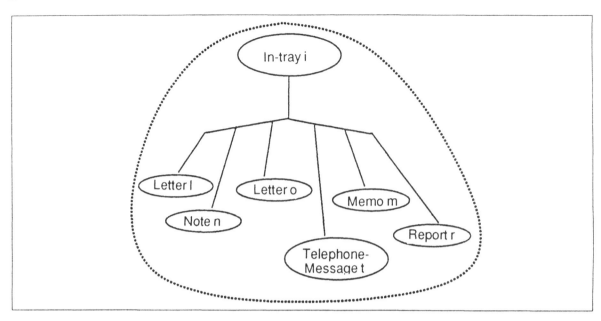

Figure 7.3: An In-tray Object Grouping

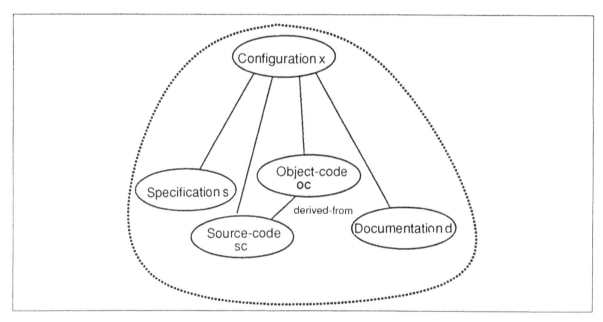

Figure 7.4: A Software Configuration Object Grouping

Figure 7.6 illustrates further complexity in version management when an object grouping such as a software configuration is considered.

7.4.4 Transparent Multimedia and Distributed Facilities

The storage of data on different media and distributed over different computer systems is becoming more and more common. The need for facilities for managing such data integrated with conventional data management is arising in many environments. GISs need support for images, OISs, IPSEs and CAD need support for figures, and OISs need support also for voice and video. In general, users do not need to be aware of the location of objects, nor of how the objects are stored. Such low level details should therefore be hidden from users and handled transparently by the system. Thus, from the viewpoint of a user or application, all the components of the presentation in Figure 7.2 may have "display-component" operations defined for them, but how this operation is implemented for each component is

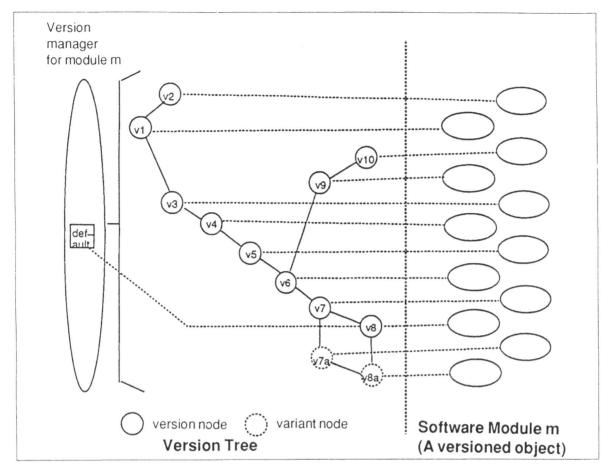

Figure 7.5: The Different Versions of a Software Module Object

hidden; in particular, the fact that the two scenes are stored on a different medium from the other components and possibly also on different computer systems may be made completely transparent.

7.4.5 Access Control Options

In some environments (e.g. OISs), responsibility for sensitive information may need to be shared or delegated. To ensure the security of such information under these conditions requires more sophisticated access control mechanisms than currently exist in traditional DBMSs. In addition, the concept of a "role" as a type of user (e.g. manager, secretary) is needed. Roles are also appropriate in an IPSE environment, in which project managers may have more access rights than project members, and may also have the right to delegate certain responsibilities. These (and other) more sophisticated access control mechanisms may be provided as options, since not all environments will require them.

7.4.6 Concurrency Options

Database transactions are typically relatively short involving only a few database accesses and simple updates. In design environments on the other hand, transactions may be lengthy, with a particular stage in the design taking hours or even days. Since co-operative working is also common in such environments, traditional concurrency control mechanisms are inappropriate – a design cannot be locked out to other co-operating designers over a long period. For example, different individuals may need to prepare different sections of the report in Figure 7.2 (or possibly even parts of the same section) at the same time. Concurrency control is another function of an OODBMS for which alternative options should be provided for selection as required by different environments.

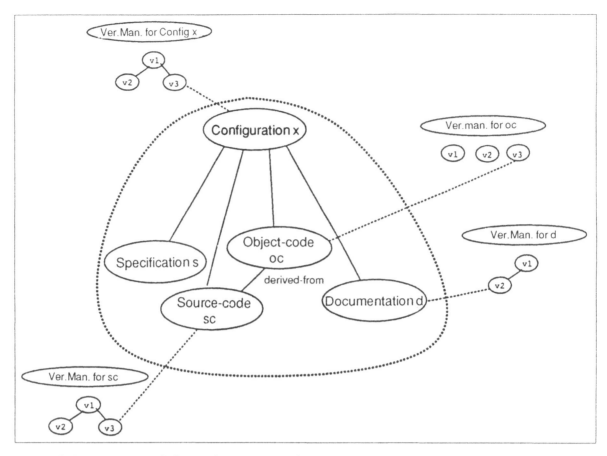

Figure 7.6: A Versioned Software Configuration Object

7.4.7 Secondary Storage Mechanisms

Secondary storage mechanisms for traditional database environments are geared towards fast retrieval of a few relatively simply structured objects from a large collection, possibly selected on the basis of certain specified relationships with other independent objects in the system (e.g. the retrieval of all students taking a particular course). These mechanisms alone are not adequate for all environments. Where small numbers of very highly structured multimedia objects are common, other mechanisms are needed. The meeting in Figure 7.2, for example, forms a complex structure which evolves as the arrangements for the meeting and the plans for the presentation take shape. It is important that the component objects should be easily accessible from the meeting object, that the different versions of the agenda and report are available as required, and that the scenes in the presentation can be located as easily as the title, abstract and duration.

7.5 Extensible And Reusable Systems

As indicated in section 7.2, current DBMSs are generally monolithic. Some OODBMSs have also been built as monolithic systems, but is now recognised that such architectures are inadequate and inappropriate for supporting a wide range of environments. While certain data management requirements are common to all or most environments, there are others which are more specialised, and systems are now being designed with extensibility and reusability in mind. This is essential for flexible and comprehensive Object Oriented data management.

There are many different software architectures which can support extensibility and reusability to a greater or a lesser extent. The reusable software in an OODBMS will be referred to in this chapter as the Object Management System (OMS), although it should be noted that this term is used to refer to only part of the reusable software in some extensible systems. In Oxborrow 1991,[9] four different approaches to extensibility are described. These are referred to as the layered approach, the modular approach, the kernel approach, and the seamless approach. In the layered approach, the reusable software is fixed and consists of a sub-system or layers of sub-systems which are shared by different specialised environments. Extensibility exists in that additional specialised environments may be built on top of the fixed shared software forming the OMS (e.g. ENCORE and GARDEN built on top of the ObServer sub-system).[10] In the modular approach, the system consists of a collection of interacting modules and all the modules are potentially reusable. Extensibility is supported by enabling different combinations of modules to be selected for particular types of environment, although some restrictions may be imposed on the way in which the modules can be combined.[11] In the kernel approach, a sub-system provides the basic OMS functions, and libraries of specialised facilities which interact with it can be selected as required. The kernel approach provides more flexibility, but at a cost. Specialised environments have to be built using special tools provided by the system. These enable the required library modules to be combined with the kernel and extended as necessary to provide a complete system.[12] The seamless approach takes this a step further, exploiting extensibility, reusability and flexibility to the full. There is no distinction between "system" and "user". Everything is potentially reusable, extensibility is possible at various levels by building on top of, and specialising, objects which exist, and any logical combination of objects is potentially possible. The seamless approach thus provides the most natural mechanism for extensibility. Any user, whether system builder, application developer or end-user, can extend the system (subject to access permissions) using the available tools. The Zenith project referred to earlier in the chapter aims to provide a system based on the seamless approach, with the system facilities being implemented as objects conforming to the Zenith object model; a prototype system is currently under development.[13]

Variations on, and combinations of, the four approaches outlined above are, of course, possible.

7.6 Conclusion

The potential market for OODBMS products is much wider than that for the current DBMS products. It is debatable whether one OODBMS could satisfy all the wide-ranging and sometimes conflicting data management requirements, but the trend towards extensible systems and software reusability makes this a possibility. What should go into a specific OODBMS product must depend on the environment(s) in which it is to be used. This suggests that future products should aim to provide a base system containing fundamental data management facilities, together with specialised data management software libraries or modules, and tools for database specialists to produce tailor-made systems oriented towards the real-world environments of the end-users.

References

[1]   M. Stonebraker *et al*, 'The Implementation of POSTGRES', in *IEEE Transactions on Knowledge and Data Engineering*, vol.2, no.1, Mar 1990, pp.125-142.

[2]   M. Atkinson, F. Bancilhon, D. DeWitt, K. Dittrich, D. Maier, S. Zdonik, 'The Object-Oriented Database System Manifesto', *Proceedings DOODS*, 1989.

[3]   W. Kim, 'Object-Oriented Databases: Definition and Research Directions', in *IEEE Transactions on Knowledge and Data Engineering*, vol.2, no.3, September 1990, pp.327-41.

[4]   M. Stonebraker *et al*, 'Third-generation Database System Manifesto', in *Proceedings IFIP TC2 Conference on Object-Oriented Databases*, 1990.

[5]   R.W. Thearle *et al*, 'An Analysis of the Data Management Requirements of Specialised Environments', submitted for publication, 1990.

[6]   O. Diaz and P.M.D. Gray, 'Semantic-rich User-defined Relationship as a Main Constructor in Object-Oriented Database', in *Proceedings IFIP TC2 Conference on Object-Oriented Databases*, 1990.

[7]   S.E. Hudson and R. King, 'Cactis, A Self-Adaptive, Concurrent Implementation of an Object-Oriented Database Management System', in *ACM Transactions on Database Systems*, vol.14, no.3, September 1989, pp.291-321.

[8]   G. Copeland, 'What if Mass Storage were Free?', *Fifth Workshop on Computer Architecture for Non-Numeric Processing*, March 1980.

[9]   E. Oxborrow *et al*, 'Object-Oriented Data Management in Specialised Environments', in *Information and Software Technology*, vol.33, no.1, January/February 1991, pp.22-30.

[10]   M.F. Hornick and S.B. Zdonik, 'A Shared, Segmented Memory System for an Object-Oriented Database', in *ACM Transactions on Office Information Systems*, vol.5, no.1, January 1987, pp.70-95.

[12]   C. Thompson *et al*, 'Open Architecture for Object-Oriented Database Systems', *Technical Report* 89-12-01, Information Technologies Lab, Texas Instruments Inc, 1989.

[13]   M.J. Carey *et al*, 'The Architecture of the EXODUS Extensible DBMS', in K.R. Dittrich and U. Dayal (eds), *Proceedings International Workshop on Object-Oriented Database Systems*, September 1986, pp.52-65.

[14]   Z.P. Kemp *et al*, 'ZENITH – An Object Management System for a Distributed Multimedia Environment', UKC Computing Laboratory Report No.94, University of Kent at Canterbury, 1991.

OBJECT MANAGEMENT
The Applications

A REVIEW OF THE SUITABILITY OF VARIOUS APPLICATIONS FOR AN 00 APPROACH

Roger Tagg
Chairman BCS Data Management Specialist Group's Working Party in Object Oriented Data Management

8.1. Introduction

While some enthusiasts see the 00 approach as the next generation for all types of computer systems application, others are aware that use of 00 techniques to date have tended to concentrate in certain application areas. This leads to the question – are there "good " areas for the 00 approach, and therefore less good ones also?

New application areas like CAD or Geographical Information Systems (GIS) are often quoted as the ideal areas for the 00 approach, together with other areas where data structures may be complex and the logic of the system relatively volatile. However, systems for such applications have already been successfully built using traditional approaches – so where does the advantage of the 00 approach arise? The answer seems to be in the ability to integrate and extend. Much of the difficulty with GIS is in combining the spatial data of the maps with the more tabular data that describes the objects on the maps. OO techniques allow a uniform approach to such "mix and match" applications, and provide good facilities for building further links to other functions (e.g. modelling pipeline flow in a network of pipes covering the geographical area on the maps).

8.2 A Categorisation Scheme for Applications When Considering an Object Oriented Approach

While some applications e.g. (CAD and GIS mentioned above) are widely regarded as "naturals" for the OO approaches, it is useful to have a more formal framework for deciding how great the pay-off of using (or converting to) an OO approach is likely to be – even if the decision is one of "when" rather than "whether or not". The framework proposed below is based on an analysis of what types of application exist in the world of target systems.

The ten dimensions introduced below are an attempt to categorise a wide range of potential computer applications. Not all the dimensions are equally critical in suggesting for or against an OO approach, although they may distinguish quite different application types.

8.3 Dimension 1 – Level of Human Interfacing

8.3.1 High

System operation is frequently punctuated dialogues with humans; the system is supporting the real-world operation "up front" or "front office". Examples: commercial TP systems such as telephone sales order taking: financial dealing systems: aircraft pilot training simulators.

8.3.2 Low

System runs for considerable periods without human intervention, either controlling some automatic process, or carrying out a long monolithic operation. Examples are spaceship onboard controller: robot controller: linear programme optimisation: commercial batch update: complex database searching.

8.3.3 Suitability

The "high" end is often associated with relatively "fixed" systems (see Dimension 4), but there is a lot of procedure tied to specific data types which encapsulates easily. Commercial TP is well covered by existing approaches, however – the data is normally in large volumes and of a tabular structure relating fairly closely to forms displayed in the human interfaces.

The "low" end is very variable – the automatic control applications are really only substituting robot interfacing for human interfacing, and so are perhaps better regarded as similar to the training simulator application type (e.g. "high"). The rest are all likely to have serial procedures acting repeatedly on a large amounts of data. Existing approaches may cover some of these areas quite well.

In summary, this dimension is not ideal as a criterion for deciding the priority of an OO approach, except in indicating the position in other Dimensions.

8.4 Dimension 2 – Required Speed of Reaction

8.4.1 High

Sub-second response time, e.g. nuclear reactor control, missile guidance. Supports a process which could go drastically wrong if not monitored and controlled very quickly.

8.4.2 Low

Off-line, background or overnight, e.g. batch reporting from a database, database reorganisation, simulation models.

8.4.3 Suitability

High speed systems are often unable to rely on the "normal" disk accessing approach, and have to keep data (much of which is transient) in main memory. Parallelism of processing would be used as far as possible to avoid bottle-necks – this could be very suitable for the OO approach. The low speed systems form a mixed bag, but many are well handled by existing approaches.

8.5 Dimension 3 – Persistence of Data

8.5.1 High

Most of the data needs to be retained from one day to the next – possibly for a year or more. Examples include "reference"-type information retrieval, insurance policy management, personnel records, laboratory test analysis.

8.5.2 Low

Most of data is only of transient interest, any retention is only for auditing or disaster analysis purposes. Examples are robotic control systems, training simulators etc.

8.5.3 Suitability

Persistence of data is not really a factor in deciding whether an application is suitable or unsuitable for the approach. But from the timing point of view, high-persistence applications would tend to be lower priority, since they would ideally need to be based on OODBMS or Persistent OOPLs (which are not yet widely available), and are also better covered by the current types of Database and CASE technology.

8.6 Dimension 4 – Volatility of Logic

8.6.1 High

Frequent changes to both procedure and data structure, including incorporation of rules as updatable elements of the system. Examples are the development stage of simulation models, CAD (where new parts/assemblies are being developed), a developing expert system or a cooperative decision support system. Spreadsheets should also be included.

8.6.2 Low

The system and data structure are virtually static, usually because the application is tied to standard accounting procedures or external legislation. Examples are Financial Accounting (though the account headings may change), Pay-rolls, Tax Return Preparation (though these may change with Tax Laws).

8.6.3 Suitability

High volatility definitely calls for an approach such as OO, where change to data structure and procedure is effected by the same sorts of means as are used for data values. Where volatility is low, there is less priority for change.

8.7 Dimension 5 – Importance of Querying

8.7.1 High

Updating procedures are fairly simple, possibly limited to table-by-table CRUD (Create Read Update Delete): but a prime purpose is to support users' queries which cannot in general be pre-packaged. Examples include bibliographic and statistical databases offered for sale, in-house management information and enquiry systems, materials or parts catalogues, office document archiving etc.

8.7.2 Low

Most systems geared to support of operational activities, including "front office" systems, on-line TP and real-time control.

8.7.3 Suitability

It is doubtful if applications with a high *ad-hoc* query element have very much to gain through an OO approach. Encapsulation tends to work against *ad-hoc* procedures, since no predefined "methods" will exist in the objects being queried and the query has to be broken down into simple reads by reference to "Repository" objects. However, on some occasions, complex objects may map more easily to user query views.

8.8 Dimension 6 – Logical Reusability

8.8.1 High

The application contains a large proportion of logic which is the same or similar to that used elsewhere. This could include other applications within the organisation; corresponding applications in other organisations; or an Application Package. Examples are Pay-roll, Accounts Payable, Inventory Control and "common" Expert Systems.

8.8.2 Low

The application is a "one-off" and is unlikely to share much logic in common with any other system. Examples are home-grown Decision Support Models; Control Systems for very specialised processes; commercial DP applications which mirror idiosyncratic clerical processes.

8.8.3 Suitability

Because of the current weakness in software reusability methods, many application systems have been built as if they were one-offs – when they could have shared many common elements. For "high" and "medium" rated applications on this dimension, the advantages of using an OO approach are potentially high, as long as the OO model reflects any potential reusability. Use of overriding with inheritance should allow systems development to be much more of an "iterative" engineering process – rather than the current expensive "start from scratch each time" style.

8.9 Dimension 7 – Complexity of Data Structures

8.9.1 High

Significant need for compound (NF^2) structures, high incidence of entity subtype hierarchies, use of "spatial" relationships where order or position is important, and also a general high density of "relationship spaghetti". Examples include most "Design" applications, especially involving assembly of constituent parts of Graphical User Interfaces; Text Retrieval systems with complex word/sentence/paragraph and Thesaurus structures; and also commercial database applications which are shared by a number of different user groups, each with different approaches to controlling the underlying real-world system.

8.9.2 Low

Only simple flat tables, arrays and strings, which includes most "personal" (i.e. non-shared) commercial applications, many real-time control systems, text handling (not including searching in full text), many expert systems.

8.9.3 Suitability

High complexity of data structures has been a problem waiting for an answer for some years, and the OO approach seems to provide a good way forward. For simpler structures there is relatively little to be gained.

8.10 Dimension 8 – Range of Media and Atomic Objects

8.10.1 High

A wide range of data types, including two or more of such types as Formatted Tables; Searchable Text; Raster Image; Vector Graphics, sound or Video Clips; and also user-defined data types such as Engineering Design parts of assemblies. Examples include Statistical/Economic Databases, Geographic Asset/Facility Management Systems, and Integrated Office Systems.

8.10.2 Low

Restricted to one of the above types, e.g. a traditional "commercial DP" application, stand-alone Bibliographic Information Retrieval, stand-alone digital mapping system etc.

8.10.3 Suitability

An OO approach allows for a consistent integrated approach to the "multi-data-type" systems. The pay-off for "low-range" applications is less, although an OO approach could still be justified on other grounds, e.g. compound data objects.

8.11 Dimension 9 – Time-dependence and Versioning

8.11.1 High

Data is subject to complex "life-cycles" in which historical states are of interest as well as current data values. Objects may change their classification over time. New objects are often derived by introducing changes to existing ones. Examples include all "Design" systems (again!), also Forecasting and Budgeting management support systems.

8.11.2 Low

Most data is of the "snapshot" variety – only the current stage is of interest.

8.11.3 Suitability

"High" applications are again fruitful ones for an OO approach, since inheritance and overriding can be used to get maximum reusability.

8.12 Dimension 10 – "Partitionability" of the Application

8.12.1 High

Can be broken down into independent and parallelisable sub-applications, e.g. on the basis of procedure groups, data types on range of data occurrences, in such a way that reference across the partitions is relatively light in volume. Examples include Specialised Servers in any cooperative system, or a commercial system which is distributable on a geographical basis (e.g. Bank Customer Accounting).

8.12.2 Low

The system is logically monolithic – most of the functions could access most of the data at any stage.

8.12.3 Suitability

Highly-partitionable applications are much more natural to analysis by an OO method, and the approach could bring benefits by encouraging the parallelisation of processing and the efficient use of small cheap hardware devices.

8.13 Summary – Positive and Negative Indicators

Collecting the findings of this analysis in ten dimensions, we are led to the following lists of indicators arguing *for* or *against* an OO approach. The numbers after each factor indicate the dimension sequence number.

8.13.1 Positive Indicators

- Real-time/sub-second response with parallelism of tasks (2).

- High rate of change in process or data structure logic (4).

- High potential for reusability of software (e.g. tailored packages or parts of similar applications elsewhere) (6).

- Data highly complex and difficult to model in conventional relational or entity-relationship terms (7).

- Wide range of basic data types and "media" (8).

- Data with significant amounts of life-cycle evolution, versioning and time-dependence (9).

- Application naturally partitionable (distribution of data or functions of specialised "servers") (10).

In summary, the ideal Object Oriented application:

- is naturally modellable as a network of cooperating logical processors.

- has an overall framework that can be envisaged as a "control system".

- is concerned with data that is still "active".

- has application logic which is either volatile or difficult to model through the normal means of functional Hierarchies, Data Flows, Procedure Dependency, Entity/Relationship structure etc.

8.13.2 Negative Indicators

- Processing follows a single serial path (2).

- Persistent data (until OODBMS market reaches maturity) (3).

- Fixed procedures and data structures represent the majority of the logic (4).

- Primarily a user query service on inactive data (5).

- A genuinely one-off application with little opportunity for software sharing and reusability (6).

- Most procedures are "multi-target" and potentially interact with many types and value ranges of data (10).

In many cases the argument is not that the OO approach could not cope, but rather that it offers little or no benefit over using existing approaches (e.g. CASE, Relational Database). In fact the OO approach may be more complex than existing approaches in some applications.

8.14 Conclusion

It is quite clear from the above analysis that different types of application vary considerably in their theoretical suitability for an OO approach. However, this analysis is only theoretical, and needs to be confirmed or corrected by a series of trials in which different approaches are applied to the same application problem in parallel. This is a task unlikely to arouse interest among commercial user organisations, but there is an opportunity here for enterprising research groups to work in conjunction with industry and government, to test the new approach out in practical solutions.

OBJECT ORIENTED TECHNIQUES IN INFORMATION ENGINEERING

Keith W. Short
JMA Information Engineering Ltd

9.1 Introduction

Object Oriented techniques have received a great deal of attention lately. A decade ago, interest in this topic was restricted to the small community of experts in Object Oriented programming and design. Today this has widened to attract the interest of developers of all kinds of systems. Object Oriented Design (OOD) and also Object Oriented Analysis (OOA) methodologies are discussed in the press, but clear direction on the appropriate use of these techniques, the relationship with techniques already in use, and how to achieve the benefits of these techniques has not been forthcoming. The role of CASE tools in connection with OO techniques is also as yet unclear.

In this chapter, we address how OO techniques fit into the Information Engineering methodology. in particular we focus on issues such as: Why is OO important to the evolution of Information Engineering? What types of problem are best suited to OO techniques? How is OOA to be related to OOD? How can full life cycle, integrated CASE exploit the new techniques? Some of the suggestions made here are of the nature of general extensions to the Information Engineering methodology, others will be illustrated by reference to what is widely acknowledged to be the fullest implementation of Information Engineering to date, the Information Engineering Facility^{tm} (IEF^{tm}) produced by Texas Instruments Inc.[1]

Information Engineering (IE) is one of the most successful system development methodologies,[2] practised by many system development groups with only slight variations. IE is also the basis for the most widely used CASE products, both in the form of component CASE tools, and the more sophisticated Integrated CASE tools. Evidence of quality and productivity gains has been substantiated repeatedly by the growing user base of Integrated CASE tools supporting Information Engineering.[3]

Why then are OO techniques receiving so much attention? We have identified at least the following reasons:

- OO programming systems and development environments are commonplace. For example, Smalltalk, once restricted to sophisticated workstations, is available for all commonly occurring platforms.

- Despite little real evidence in practice, it is widely held that OO techniques can improve reusability. Standard definitions of objects can be made available which encourage reuse in an analogous way to, say, reusable electronic components in electrical engineering. Estimates exist that as much as 90% of code could be built in this way.[4]

- Older process oriented methodologies are no longer adequate for the types of systems which are required today. For example, Yourdon points out that process oriented methodologies matched the input-process-output paradigm of the 1970s and early 1980s, but these do not match the event-driven style demanded by modern window-driven systems where as much as 75% of the code is concerned with the human interface.[5]

So, if OO techniques have benefits over previous approaches, should all development projects now switch to the new approach (the "revolutionist" position)? Or are the benefits of the OO approach available in addition to those of traditional techniques for special categories of systems (the "synthesist" position)? Since IE has always had an important emphasis on data modelling, we believe that the answer lies in the use of IE together with new techniques associated with the world of OO. What then, are the categories of systems which can benefit from this approach?

9.2 Enterprise Wide Integrated Systems

We believe that the answer lies in the identification of methodology techniques which match the focus of the problem to be addressed. To understand what this means in the context of adding new techniques to IE, we need to analyse what is meant by system categories.

A diagram from the Information Strategy Planning stage of Information Engineering helps to illustrate this concept: the Business System Architecture diagram (Figure 9.1).

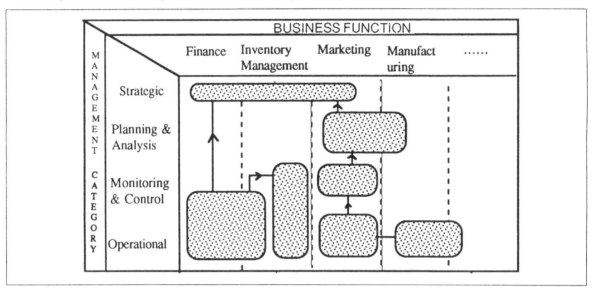

Figure 9.1: Business System Architecture Diagram

The shaded areas of Figure 9.1 represent business systems and the principal dependencies between them. This diagram is used to show how proposed and existing systems cover the categories of management requirements across each of the business functions, The system categories indicate the kinds of support to the business function that each system provides.

*   **Strategic** support is typified by unpredictable, judgemental interaction with data from a variety of sources, often historical and sometimes external.

*   **Planning and Analysis** support is typified by the analysis of trends and exceptions, involving "what-ifs" and statistical modelling of extracts from operational data.

*   **Monitoring and Control** systems are the routine analyses and reports which have a long lifetime and deal with large volumes of structured operational data.

*   **Operational** support is typified by high volume, time critical using predefined transactions and processing relatively small areas of often large databases.

Currently, the IE methodology and there IE-based CASE tools have little to offer to the development of Strategic or Planning and Analysis system types. The processing pertinent to these systems, and their data characteristics, have not been addressed by the current generation of CASE products, and require a different approach to their automation than those in the lower half of Figure 9.1.[6] Methodologies for these systems need to address issues arising from the increased degrees of unstructuredness in these management levels, such as unpredictable and rapidly changing specifications, advanced modelling such as planning or econometric analysis, and the development of highly interactive, graphical human-computer interfaces.

For these reasons, systems towards the top of the diagram are also said to be more difficult to formalise compared with those in the lower half. This means that techniques for dealing with hard-to-formalise requirements need to be introduced if systems are to be built in these categories. Examples would be decision analysis and knowledge engineering. A key factor here is that it is through development of these categories that competitive breakthrough can be attained, as operational levels become widely automated.

Monitoring and Control, and Operational systems have been the main target for development methods and CASE tools. It is the lower levels of the diagram which form the areas in which IE and IE-based CASE excel. Operational systems often provide the underlying databases for exploitation by higher level systems. This means that data and process distribution becomes increasingly significant as an enabling technology. Few of today's CASE tools can support this technology (although a few of the CASE vendors have announced their intention to do so for limited form of cooperative processing during 1991).

To summarise these points, extensions to IE and IE-based CASE tools are required to build systems which have the following characteristics:

- Semantically rich conceptual models to model complex problems and which support techniques for dealing with hard-to-formalise requirements, such as knowledge engineering.

- Flexible, reusable conceptual and design components to develop systems which support rapid construction of applications with evolving requirements.

- Concepts to assist the development of highly interactive systems with sophisticated graphical interfaces.

- Concepts to assist the development of distributed, cooperative applications using databases from the operational layer of the business system architecture.

The first three of these points directly correspond to the areas of software development to which the OO paradigm has brought benefits. Many knowledge engineering toolsets and environments adopt an OO paradigm for their design and problem models. Extensibility and reusability are major factors in the ability of OO techniques to support the development of flexible systems. The power of the OO paradigm fo developing graphical systems is well documented.

An example is that of the manufacturing company wishing to increase system support for automating its manufacturing process. A real world entity type such as *machine* may be modelled in an operational information system using IE techniques. Construction of a graphical system to support planning and monitoring of resources is required. In this case, the extract to be visualised or subjected to analysis will be derived from the IE model, but development of the knowledge base and human interface may be best performed using Object Oriented techniques, combined with a predefined set of object classes. For example, in a higher level planning system, instances of the *machine* above may be visualised as icons on a factory floor layout, with dynamic behaviour simulated through the use of alternate scheduling knowledge bases.

A problem arises as a result of the last point above. If the competitive breakthrough, or secondary level, systems are to use operational systems and databases which gave been produced (or generated by I-CASE tools) from conceptual models built using IE techniques (e.g. entity relationship diagrams and process decomposition diagrams), how should the preferred OO techniques relate to these existing models to ensure integrated systems are produced? Before addressing this question, we need to study how OO techniques and IE relate today.

9.3 IE and OO Techniques

The following characteristics are regarded as features of the OO paradigm:

- Abstraction

- Encapsulation

- Inheritance

- Polymorphism

- Reusability

- Extensibility

Strictly speaking inheritance is a form of abstraction, the generalisation abstraction, but it is common for these to be separately addressed. Also, it could be argued that reusability and extensibility are not characteristics of the OO paradigm, but examples of benefits provided by characteristics such as encapsulation and inheritance of operations. Debate ensues as to how many of these characteristics are mandatory to be classified as "Object Oriented", and which are optional. For example, purists argue that Ada is merely "object based" because it supports encapsulation and abstraction, but not inheritance.

IE is primarily used on problem spaces where the aspects of **process** (what is done within the problem space) and **data** (what the processes are operating on) are given about equal emphasis.[7] The techniques reflect this, which leads to projects structured differently from those which might be following a pure OO analysis approach. However, because IE incorporates some well developed data modelling techniques, aspects of the above OO characteristics are supported.

- Abstraction – Level of abstraction are supported by several IE techniques. Aggregation abstraction is offered through activity decomposition diagrams, in which functions are decomposed into processes, which are then further decomposed. On the data side, subject area decomposition is supported by entity relationship diagrams, in which subject areas are hierarchical aggregates of entity types and other subject areas. The classification abstraction is supported by the concept of an entity type.

- Encapsulation – This is not well supported by IE or IE-based CASE tools. This is usually taken to mean information hiding, in which details of entity type attributes and operations are hidden, with interaction restricted to publicly available operation specifications.

- Inheritance – This is supported by IE techniques through the concept of entity subtype hierarchies. In IEF, these can be visualised both as hierarchies or nested boxes within entity types on the entity relationship diagram. Multiple partitioning of subtype hierarchies provide for richer models, effectively offering an AND-OR graph of types within one hierarchy. Inheritance is limited to attributes and relationships.

- Polymorphism and extensibility are not supported currently by IE or any implementation of it.

To satisfy the objectives stated in the previous section, it is possible to conceive how new techniques and concepts can be added to those currently in IE which have originated from the need to develop operational, transaction based database systems.

9.4 Extending IE Analysis Techniques

Recall that our primary objective is to produce semantically rich, flexible conceptual models. Given that IE already supports a rich set of modelling techniques, how can these be extended to build the systems discussed above, and how are these related to the techniques familiar to users of the OO paradigm?

9.4.1 Further Abstractions

Two suggestions are made for increasing the support for abstraction in IE – aggregation as a relationship type, and instances. In the preceding section, it was said that IE supports aggregation using various decomposition techniques. These are examples of aggregation at the application level. Support for aggregation as a meta concept is not provided within IE. For example, within IE conceptual models, relationship between entity types are frequently identified by the pattern: Each **A** *contains* many **B**s/Each **B** *is part of* one **A**. A is therefore said to be a "container class" for Bs. Since many standard and stereotypical operations are defined for container classes, a new line type could be provided to distinguish the aggregation from other relationships.

Support for named instances of entity types has not been provided by IE methodologies and CASE tools. Often, this results in clumsy models (e.g. **HM Government** becomes the sole stance of the type **Government** with name = "HM Government"). Stereotypical (unnamed) instances are supported in IE on those diagrams dealing with process specification (e.g. the Process Logic Diagram[8]) but these are not permitted alongside the type specifications. Adding a symbol to represent both named and unnamed instances would add modelling power to IE.

9.4.2 Methods – Further Normalisation of the Conceptual Model

One of the most obvious distinctions between IE and OO techniques is the encapsulation of operations within the definition of objects. This represents an additional normalisation of the conceptual model over the normalisation of data provided by entity relationship techniques. With existing IE techniques, an elementary process is identified which typically directly expresses the effects it has on several related entity types (although it may use lower level reusable routines). This often leads to duplicated logic in elementary processes which deal with similar sets of related entity types, and the problems of maintenance normally associated with unnormalised information.

We are experimenting with a new form of IE which permits the definition of methods as part of the definition of entity types. These can be inherited, thus providing polymorphism within inheritance hierarchies.

Note that the concept of "success unit" by which integrity of the data model is maintained across a set of lower level operations is still required. This is part of the role of an elementary process in IE. Few OO methods have address this issue thoroughly.

9.4.3 Declarative Analysis

Pursuing the concept of further normalisation of the process model, it is possible to identify other parts of process (and method) definitions which are often duplicated in many processes because they represent business rules, constraints and policies. For example, Figure 9.2 shows a simple fragment of an entity relationship diagram showing the relationship between **customers** and **orders**.

The business rule shown expresses some additional constraint on membership beyond that which can be depicted graphically. It also shows that these rules inter-relate, i.e. there must exist some rule which defines what is meant by *good* and *bad* customers.

Normalisation reminds us that components of the conceptual model should be stored once (e.g. not repeated within every process or method which deals with orders and customers), preferably defined in the context of the data model component to which they refer. For example, the rule in Figure 9.2 should be held as an integrity constraint on the cardinality of the relationship shown.

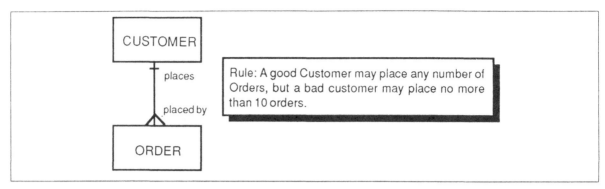

Figure 9.2: Relationship between Customers and Orders

Thus, normalisation of process models continues from the allocation of entity actions to methods (9.4.2 above) to declarative specifications of the business rules, constraints and policies. This has the following benefits.

- Declarative specifications expressed in terms of conceptual data model elements should be closer to the business, and therefore easier to verify than fragmented versions of them spread inside nested procedural logic.

- Greater flexibility is gained since policies and rules change more frequently than data models and process structures (i.e. change and maintenance is easier).[9]

- Greater independence of analysis from design is enabled, since there is less opportunity to taint the conceptual model with implementation details.

- The finer granularity obtained from process specifications as sets of rules, enables tight integration with graphical specifications such as the Entity Life Cycle Diagram and the Process Logic Diagram. This is illustrated in Figure 9.3.

We are experimenting with a version of IEF which supports the definition of business policies, rules and constraints as parts of the data model, and expresses processes as pre-condition rules (when and what is required) and post-condition rules (outcomes). This is called Declarative Analysis. The effect is to satisfy many of the goals of CASE tools to support higher level systems in the Business System Architecture (Figure 9.1). Combined with the encapsulation features as above, this enables extensible processes and methods, greater flexibility and semantically richer conceptual models.

9.4.4 Multiple Inheritance

IE and IEF today support entity type hierarchies using the subtype concept. OO methodologies often advocate inheritance from more than one "parent" forming an inheritance lattice instead of a hierarchy. Judicious use of this concept can enrich models, and encourage further reusability, but it introduces two main problems:

- Naming conflicts, as methods and attributes from different inheritance paths in the lattice may have the same name.

- The embedded subtype notation used in IE and IEF, which graphically serves to illustrate single inheritance very well, will need to be extended to represent inheritance relationships as a new line type in the Entity Relationship Diagram.

Note that the OO techniques described can be integrated with the existing IE techniques (i.e. the underlying meta model provides for both perspectives). This provides the opportunity to build systems where the OO approach is more appropriate, which can then be integrated with systems built using traditional IE.

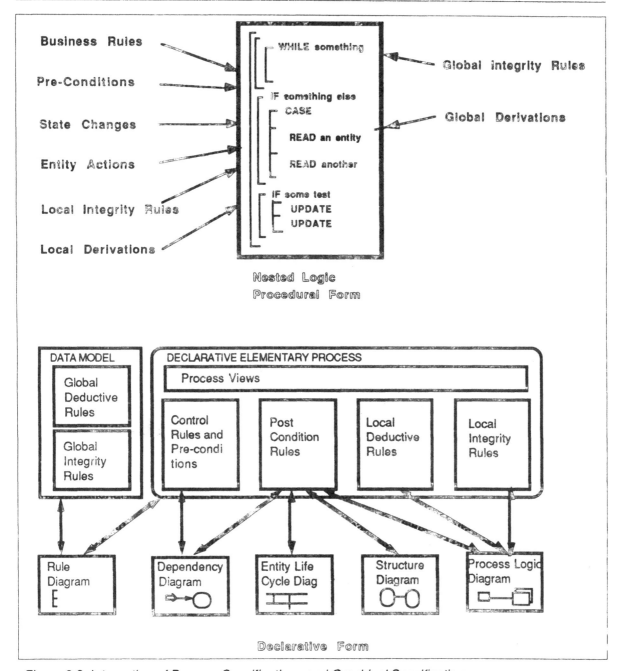

Figure 9.3: Integration of Process Specifications and Graphical Specifications

This enables projects to choose the approach best suited to the focus of the problem on hand. This does not mean that projects with a small overlap with existing IE models will use the techniques in the same way, or follow the same project structure as IE projects. For example, greater emphasis will be put on the use of event specification, dependency analysis and entity life cycle analysis, all essentially OO techniques, than is common today.

9.5 Object Oriented Design with the IEF

IEF provides for design tools which are tightly integrated into the development process, performing the role of adding target environment-specific (or a generic class of environments, such as screen-based TP systems) implementation strategies to conceptual model elements. This activity tends to be iterative and evolutionary. In the current version of IEF, these design tasks require minimum knowledge of the actual TP system for which design is performed.

In subsequent releases, IEF will add to its productivity and quality gains by further assisting the design activity using knowledge bases of design skills,. These are applied to the elementary processes in the conceptual model to produce high quality, first-cut implementation strategies for those processes. These implementation strategies are known as Design Stereotypes in IEF.

These Design Stereotypes held in the knowledge bases can be regarded as a predefined set of objects to be used to create implementation strategies for processes in the conceptual model. They are selected either manually, or in later versions of IEF, using an inference process known as analogical reasoning, and customised by the designer (see Figure 9.4). They are capable of generating large quantities of design detail, such as system structuring and flows, screen layouts, command handling etc.

The effect of this is a further de-skilling of the design activity. In fact, the designer is performing Object Oriented design by using the predefined object classes, but is selecting and customising them using design tools relevant to the problem domain (Screen Design tool, Dialog Flow Diagram etc). This offers great potential for improving productivity and quality, but at the expense of non-standard processing relegated to calls to external routines, or explicitly added with procedural logic.

This approach can be extended for a wider class of application types. Within our research group, we

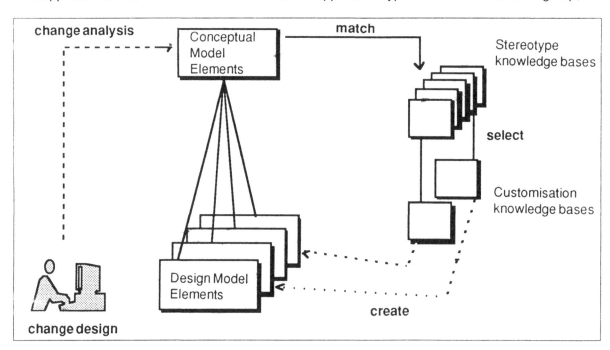

Figure 9.4: Analogical reasoning

have built knowledge bases for the design of window-based applications, and are working on knowledge bases and suitable integrated design tools for graphics based applications necessary to support the development of visualisation systems as described in section 9.2 above. Other knowledge bases and toolsets are planned for constructing classes of knowledge based systems as application components, and distributed processing applications. Both of these are examples of application areas in which OO techniques are widely used. In each of these toolsets, knowledge of the OO design and construction techniques which they represent, may be hidden from most users of the IEF. As OO techniques gain wider acceptance for a wider class of applications, IEF could support generic OO design tools, such as those proposed by Booch,[10] or Schlaer and Mellor[11] in their methodologies.

9.6 Summary

In this chapter we have identified categories of systems which go beyond the operational support of enterprises. To build these systems requires flexible, rigorous, business oriented semantically rich conceptual models and powerful design toolsets. These system categories involve specifications which call for flexible, highly interactive, often knowledge based processing. Object oriented analysis and design techniques have excelled in the construction of this kind of system. We proposed that, though IE is a powerful conceptual modelling methodology, additional techniques could be added to support the construction of richer models, many of these identifiable as OO techniques.

In the IEF tool, design is assisted by knowledge bases of design skills. It is our belief that this combination of stereotype-based objects for specific classes of application, with appropriate domain-specific design and customisation tools, will significantly assist companies to create the higher level system categories referred to in section 9.2 which support the development of competitive breakthrough, integrated systems, with minimal requirement to upgrade the skills of existing developers.

9.7 Acknowledgements

The author would like to thank colleagues at JMA Information Engineering Ltd and Texas Instruments for ideas contributed to this chapter.

The views expressed in this chapter are those of the author, and should not be construed as a statement of direction for either JMA Information Engineering Ltd or Texas Instruments with regard to Information Engineering and the Information Engineering Facility[tm].

Information Engineering Facility and IEF are trademarks of Texas Instruments Inc.

References

[1] Information on the IEF[tm] can be obtained from: JMA Information Engineering Ltd., Littleton Road, Ashford, Middlesex, England, TW15 1TZ.
[2] I. Macdonald, 'Information Engineering', in T.W. Olle, H. Sol, A. Verign-Stuart (eds.) *CRIS 86 – Improving the Practice*, North Holland, 1986; J. Martin, *Information Engineering*, volumes 1, 2, 3 and 4, Prentice Hall, New Jersey, 1990; C. Finkelstein, *An Introduction to Information Engineering*, Addison-Wesley, Sydney, 1990.
[3] Gartner Group, *A Survey of the CASE Market – User Satisfaction*, September 1990.
[4] P.G. Bassett, *Frame Based Software Engineering*, IEEE Software, July 1987.
[5] E. Yourdon, 'Auld Lang Syne', *Byte*, October 1990.
[6] G.A. Gorry, M.S. Scott Morton, 'A Framework for Management Information Systems', *Sloane Management Review*, Vol. 13, No. 1, Fall 1971.
[7] K.W. Short, 'Methodology Integration: The Evolution of Information Engineering', *Information and Software Technology*, CASE Special Issue, November 1991.
[8] J. Martin, *Information Engineering*, volumes 1, 2, 3 and 4, Prentice Hall, New Jersey, 1990; C. Finkelstein, '*An Introduction to Information Engineering*, Addison-Wesley, Sydney, 1990.
[9] P. Loucopoulos, P.J. Layzell, 'Improving Information System Development and Evolution using a Rule-based Paradigm', *Software Engineering Journal*, September 1989.
[10] G. Booch, *Object Oriented Design with Applications*, Benjamin/Cummings Publishing Company, Inc. 1990.
[11] S. Schlaer, S. Mellor, *Object Oriented Systems Analysis – Modelling the World with Data*, Prentice Hall, Englewood Cliffs, New Jersey, 1990.

OBJECT ORIENTED METHODOLOGIES AND GEOGRAPHICAL INFORMATION SYSTEMS – A NATURAL PARTNERSHIP?

Robert Barr
Urban Research and Policy Evaluation Regional Research Laboratory, University of Manchester

10.1 Introduction

The term Geographical Information System has been applied to a wide range of computing environments that provide facilities for the storage, retrieval, display and analysis of data with a spatial component. While the diversity of such systems makes generalisations difficult, it is generally acknowledged that spatial data, in either textual or graphical form presents particular processing challenges that are well met by an Object Oriented approach. As a result, Object Oriented methodologies, including Object Oriented graphics, programming, analysis and databases have received considerable attention in the geographical information systems literature recently. This explosion of interest is not yet matched by many practical products or implemented systems, however, the first vendors are beginning to enter the marketplace. This chapter argues that the most important part of the approach will be the application of Object Oriented analysis to define suitable data models and to encourage data and method sharing across Open Systems compliant networks connecting diverse hardware platforms running both existing applications and novel software.

Over recent years there has been an explosive increase in the availability of geographic data. Typical examples include Landsat or SPOT satellite imagery, digital versions of the Ordnance Survey's map series, population census data, and associated boundary information, and comprehensive address files such as the Post Office's postal address file. There has been a recognition in this, and in many other countries, that the availability of geographic information in unprecedented volumes allows a new range of problems to be tackled. Many of the potential solutions were not economically feasible in the past. Governments have recognised the importance of geographic data handling technologies and have responded by the funding and encouragement of many national initiatives. Characteristically, in the UK, the response has been a long string of government reports, matched by few actions. The House of Lords Select Committee on Science and Technology published its report on Remote Sensing and Digital Mapping in 1983.[1] This report highlighted the need to develop enabling technologies to allow the effective exploitation of such data and called on the government to respond. The government's response was to establish a second committee chaired by Lord Chorley to sit under the auspices of the Department of the Environment. This reported in 1987 with a handbook entitled *The Handling of Geographic Information* that again highlighted the great variety of applications ranging from land use planning, through the management of utility networks, the co-ordination of street works, operations such as the administration of local land searches to the analysis of demographic patterns for social planning or marketing applications.[2] Unfortunately, while succeeding in demonstrating the widespread applicability of Geographic data handling technology, the report didn't persuade government that the exploitation of such technologies required significant public funding, a fact that had not gone unnoticed in the USA, Australia or the Netherlands.[3]

Geographical Information Systems(GISs) have been defined as "... extensible computer facilities that handle data pertaining to areas of ground or to individuals living or working within those areas ...".[4] This definition is important and helpful because it does not suggest that a GIS is necessarily a single software package. It implies rather that it is an amalgam of hardware platform (or platforms), geographically referenced data and appropriate software. It is to this broader definition that the applicability of Object Oriented methodology needs to be addressed.

10.2 The Nature of GIS

Because of the widespread interest in Geographical Information Systems the term is being applied increasingly loosely to a wide range of systems. (Perhaps much in the same way as the term "Object Oriented" is increasingly seen as a Good Housekeeping seal of approval and is being used in a cavalier fashion by vendors and users.) For a software package to be fully recognised as a GIS it needs to have three areas of capability:

- Facilities to enable the handling of geographical references, such as locational co-ordinates or place name information such as street addresses.

- The capability of handling graphical data in map form and of automating aspects of map production.

- The ability to carry out spatial analytical functions such as polygon overlay or network analysis. The results of such an analysis are either a new map (in the case of polygon overlay), whose geometrical form and attached attributes are inherited from a pair of input maps, or, in the case network analysis, new attributes attached to existing graphical entities.

Geographical information systems that qualify under these three headings are sometimes called "fully functional GIS", to distinguish them from products that may be simply spatial databases or automated cartography tools. Fully functional GISs are built around two fundamental graphical models. Raster GIS operate on gridded data where the resolution of the individual grid cell may vary from very small for high resolution aerial photography or satellite imagery, to kilometres across for a highly generalised grid map. All the analytical operations on a Raster GIS take advantage of the regular data structure and the advantages it offers for certain operations. Raster GIS are weaker, however, in operations that require cartographic accuracy rather than ease of analysis and are concerned mainly with operations on points and areas. By contrast GISs built to handle the vector data model can operate equally easily on points lines and areas, have a richer set of analytical capabilities (though these may be more cumbersome than in a raster system), can produce output of production cartographic quality and have more flexibility in the way in which they handle attribute data attached to spatial objects.

Recently the relative merits of raster and vector systems have been recognised by their respective vendors and there has been a trend towards building more raster data handling capability in to vector systems and vice versa. It is important to recognise the central role of the graphics data structure in a GIS. Unlike conventional drawing packages or less sophisticated CAD, systems where graphical data has attributes attached that simply show how it should be displayed, in a GIS graphical objects need to be structured to represent objects in the real world. The graphical structure of a GIS object needs to accommodate both the representation of the object on chapter or screen and the depiction of objects that reflect entities whose attributes are held in the underlying database.

For example, a single line segment on an Ordnance survey map may constitute a single graphical entity but it may form part of several logical entities. It may simultaneously represent a legal property boundary, a physical edge of a building and part of an administrative boundary. A GIS needs to be able to structure its graphical data to represent both existing logical entities and ones derived from further analysis. An instance may be the generation of least cost routes through a network, following the analysis the results may be stored as attributes of the links making up the best route.

10.3 The Design of GIS

The relationship between the core software, the graphical data model and the attribute database has become the fundamental issue in GIS design. One of the earliest, and still most successful, GIS designs, was that of ARC/INFO.[5] This took the route of using a proprietary relational database, INFO and implementing a customised file structure for holding graphical data as a series of map sheets, or tiles, which could be abutted, merged or have arbitrary regions cut out of them. Such an approach uses the strength of the database technology where it is appropriate but does not suffer the crippling performance overheads of storing the graphical data in the same way. A characteristic of GISs is the very large volume of graphical/spatial data compared with the size of the attribute data sets. These problems are frequently greater for raster than for vector data, but with either, the handling of large data volumes is the limiting factor in GIS performance. For rapid retrieval of spatial data (when panning or zooming over a large area, for example) it is important that this graphical database should be indexed in at least two dimensions and ideally three (or four if the temporal dimension is needed, which is now frequently the case).

Two further systems provided alternative approaches to the graphics problem. Deltamap, now known as Genamap,[6] was designed around a strategy for handling graphics in R-trees (a data structure suitable for indexing arbitrary rectangles) mapped closely to the physical file structure in UNIX systems. This has achieved a seamless scaleless map database with high performance. However, taking the UNIX toolbox approach only very simple facilities are provided for the manipulation of attribute data and an efficient interface to external relational databases is provided.

A third approach was taken by the designers of System 9, a GIS now marketed by Prime. They opted for a "clean" approach of storing both geometric and graphical data in a relational database, Empress 32, and using an industry standard GKS graphics interface. However, the first generation of System 9 suffered severe performance problems. These were overcome by using the "bulk" data type that is a feature of Empress. The geometric data was stored in a proprietary format and was effectively treated by Empress as a set of binary large objects that were operated on by the core code of the application. The graphics performance was enhanced by scrapping the GKS interface and writing a new graphics kernel optimised to the SUN 3 (so much for standards!).

10.4 GIS Developments

Each of the three products listed above, that are considered by their vendors to be leading edge contenders in the general purpose fully functional GIS market, has suffered because of limitations in the software tools available to the designers. The demands of handling large quantities of spatial data with a need for multidimensional indexing has stretched existing relational database technology to breaking point. It is difficult to combine a high level analytic capability with the capacity for very large numbers of simple search and query transactions. It is interesting that for applications that need to be able to support a large transactional load both IBM and ICL offer products built around more conventional hierarchical databases. The products all have user interfaces that, though improving, are poor by comparison with the latest offerings using Motif or Windows and careful design. None of the products lend themselves to the development of simple, efficient and inexpensive stand-alone applications.

Yet there are further demands coming from GIS users. There is a demand for better integration of vector and raster models. Appetites whetted by demonstration products such as the Domesday book[7] are looking forward to multi-media GIS[8] that will integrate still photographs, sound and full video into GIS. Users are looking for better interworking particularly with the more powerful tools becoming available on PCs. An expectation is growing that the transparent exchange of data across networks should be becoming routine (rather than unreliable and cumbersome as it is now). Fears grow concerning accuracy, reliability and timeliness issues in data particularly when updating map bases or combining attributes from different sources. Users are expecting better user interfaces that come closer to the standards set by leading edge PC software. Users are expecting custom applications to be built reliably from existing components and taking advantage of existing data. (It has been estimated that data costs can account for over 70% of the cost of any GIS project.)

10.5 Object Orientation – The Holy Grail?

When such a large set of expectations are raised it is unfair to expect any one methodology to be able to meet them. The GIS community is beginning to pin its hopes on object orientation. The more mature observers do not expect magical results by tomorrow and realise that we have an agenda for the 1990s and beyond, but given that most of our present tools have their roots in the 1970s that is to be expected.

GIS is inherently concerned with objects. When we refer to "structured" graphical data as opposed to "spaghetti", we are talking about graphical objects represented as points, lines and arcs to which attributes are attached. We are used to the idea that different objects have different appropriate "methods". The fundamental "method" of polygon overlay leads directly to the creation of a new "object" that inherits its characteristics from the objects it was derived from. However, such objects are still relatively dumb, they will not warn the user whether the polygons that are being overlaid can be sensibly combined. Most existing GIS products have been developed largely in FORTRAN or, more recently C. The shift to using C++ and adopting the broader paradigm of Object Oriented programming is slow at present.

The lowest level of object orientation in GIS is the move to C++ and associated databases that support C++. An example of a system, which at present is replicating the functionality of existing GIS systems using an Object Oriented approach is the SIRO-SPOT system[9] that uses the Ontos Object Oriented database. Ontos claims a 500 fold increase in performance over relational products in certain applications. This product also uses an X-Windows user interface to provide a high degree of platform independence.

A much more ambitious venture which seeks to develop an Object Oriented toolkit not just to replicate existing GIS functionality, but to attack hitherto difficult problems is Small World's product.[10] This product includes its own Object Oriented implementation language – Magik. This approach is likely to allow the development of specific GIS solutions to particular problems. The developers have used the Object Oriented approach to tackle the specific problems of the temporal dimension in GIS and of automated and semi automated data capture and data structuring. The Object Oriented approach, in this case, is allowing the rapid development of applications that tackle significant shortcomings in existing products and important and costly bottle-necks in the productive use of GIS.

A third straw in the wind is the use of a Smalltalk based system[11] as a front end to a large IBM mainframe based GIS. In this case the ability to retrieve modify and replace objects from the mainframe environment using a PC based application is pointing to a method of working that can be expected to become more common in future.

While these three examples are of real software handling real problems there are many more pencil and chapter exercises taking place at the moment. Geographical data and its attributes are being rethought in an Object Oriented analytical framework. This intellectual data modeling work is an important precursor to the implementation of real systems as new Object Oriented databases become available and interworking over networks becomes more common. At the same time new languages are being investigated, the GIS community has already been working on spatial extensions to SQL but these efforts are now being combined with the assessment of Object Oriented extensions to SQL.

10.6 Conclusion

The range of Object Oriented methodologies, including programming methods, methods of data analysis, methods of object storage and transmission across networks promise a revolution in geographical data handling over the next decade which will be as significant as the use of GIS has been in the last. To bring these opportunities to fruition close collaboration between computing professionals, geographic analysts and end users will be required to ensure that the new technologies offer real solutions to real problems.

A natural partnership? Certainly!

References

[1]   H.M.S.O. *Select Committee on Science and Technology Remote Sensing and Digital Mapping, House of Lords*, Session 1983-84 1st report, London, 1983.

[2]   Department of the Environment, *Handling Geographic Information: Report of the Committee of Enquiry Chaired by Lord Chorley*, HMSO, London, 1987.

[3]   Easterfield, M.E., Newell, R.G. and Theriault, D.G., 'Version Management in GIS – Applications and Techniques', *Proceedings EGIS '90, Amsterdam April 1990*, EGIS Foundation, Utrecht, 1990.

[4]   Rhind D.W., 'Geographical Information Systems in Britain', Wrigley N. and Bennett R.J. (eds.), *Quantitative Geography*, Routledge Kegan Paul, London, 1981.

[5]   Peuquet D. and Marble D., 'ARC/INFO: an example of a contemporary geographic information system', Peuquet D. and Marble D. (eds.) *Introductory Readings in Geographic Information Systems*, Taylor and Francis, London, 1990.

[6]   Reed C.N., 'Deltamap – just another new GIS?', *Proceedings second international symposium on spatial data handling*, July 5-10, 1986 Seattle, Washington, U.S.A., International Geographical Union, Williamsville N.Y, 1986.

[7]   Rhind D.W. and Openshaw S., 'The BBC Domesday: A Nationwide GIS for $4448', *Proceedings Auto Carto 8*, ACSM, Baltimore, 1987.

[8]   Lewis S. and Rhind D, 'Multimedia Geographical Information Systems', *Mapping Awareness '91: proceedings of the conference held in London*, February 1991,pp. 311 – 322, Blenheim Online, London, 1990.

[9]   Halstead M., Mackenzie H., Milne P., Milton S. and Smith J., 'A Spatial Object Toolkit', *Proceedings URPIS 18 Canberra November 21-23 1990*, Canberra, 1990.

[10]   Chance, A. Newell, R.G. and Theriault, D.G., 'An Object Oriented GIS – Issues and Solutions', *Proceedings EGIS '90, Amsterdam April 1990*, EGIS Foundation, Utrecht, 1990.

[11]   Noparstak B. (ed), 'Object GPG', *Scoop* Vol. 3 No. 2, Digitalk Inc., Los Angeles, 1990.

CASE STUDY: COMPUTER-AIDED CONTROL SYSTEM DESIGN

J.M. Maciejowski and C.Y. Tan
Cambridge University Engineering Department, Cambridge

11.1 Introduction

We review the facilities which a CAD environment needs to offer engineering designers, and more specifically to control engineers. We suggest that such facilities are best provided by having a "smart" database management system as the core of a CAD environment. Such a DBMS should be Object Oriented in a loose sense, though it may be best not to insist on strict object orientation. We describe an environment which we have developed, which is based on these ideas; it is implemented by extending Prolog with database-like capabilities, to form a "database programming environment". Navigation around the database is simplified by an application-specific interface.

Most areas of engineering design can benefit from computer assistance. Electromagnetic devices, such as motors, for instance, require complicated field calculations to check whether a particular combination of mechanical layout and electrical windings will deliver the required power at the right speed, without getting too hot, weighing too much, being too bulky, and costing too much. VLSI chips need to have their silicon etched and doped with impurities in such a way that the individual gates perform their functions correctly, and that they are correctly connected to each other, without getting any connections crossed; millions of gates may be needed on each chip, so this task clearly demands automation. The chips must be connected together onto "boards" in such a way that other requirements are met; for example, they should not emit too much electromagnetic interference when they are operating – predicting this before manufacture is another task which requires computer assistance.

If you consider the design of a complete aircraft, it is easy to see that there is a host of design decisions which have to be taken on various aspects of the aircraft, and which have to be consistent with each other. The structure (airframe) must be strong enough to support the payload, plus the weight of engines and fuel, not forgetting its own weight. The design of components, such as the engines or the undercarriage, therefore has consequences for other parts of the design. Apart from meeting the basic requirements, the resulting aircraft must be sufficiently reliable and efficient. Computer assistance is virtually essential at every stage of the design.

We have worked on the problem of designing control systems, so we shall use that application as an example later in this chapter. We should therefore say what we understand a control system to be. Examples of control systems occur in many industries and devices. An autopilot, which keeps an aircraft flying at the correct speed, altitude and course, is an example of a control system. So is the feedback system which keeps a chemical process running at the correct temperature and pressure, or (a very challenging design example) the mechanism which keeps the light spot focussed on the disk in your portable CD-player as you jog. Although each of these examples is taken from different technological areas, they can all be designed by using a common underlying theory – control theory. There is therefore a distinct niche of engineering activity, occupied by control engineers.

11.2 Requirements of Engineering Design

Computer support for engineering design must satisfy some requirements which are common to all specialisations. Most important is the fact that *design* must be supported, as well as analysis. In spite of being based on science and technology, engineering design is a truly creative activity; the implication of this is that the activity of an engineering designer cannot be fully predicted in advance, and that a designer's use of computer assistance may occur in a largely random way. A CAD environment which forces a designer to follow a prescribed sequence of steps may not match the design process well. (At some level of activity such a prescribed sequence may well be appropriate, for example to ensure that Quality Assurance procedures have been adhered to. It may also be appropriate to *advise* a particular sequence, rather than insist on it.)

Another universal requirement is that of supporting complex numerical computation, possibly with graphical interpretation of the results.

In the course of any design, a significant quantity of data will be generated. This data should be available conveniently to the designer; ideally a CAD system should check that the data it accumulates about a design task is mutually consistent. It should be easy to "pick up" a chunk of data (describing a proposed design of a jet engine, for example) and submit it to some number-crunching algorithm.

Of course, when we say "designer" we may actually mean a team of people. Certainly in the aerospace and electronics industries design teams may be very large, and design projects may extend over months or even years. Design data should be available to various members of such a team, and it should be possible to track the history of various design decisions (for "quality audits", for example).

It is our belief that the key to meeting these requirements in a CAD system is the development of a sufficiently "smart" database management system, which should be the core to which the other components needed in a CAD system can be attached. This belief is no longer controversial, and has been one of the stimuli to the development of Object Oriented database management systems.[1]

How "smart" does such a DBMS have to be? In particular, how much "smarter" than a conventional relational DBMS? First of all, it must be able to represent engineering data in a reasonably natural way. If you have an aircraft with four engines, each of which has two combustion chambers, then it should be able to represent this fairly easily. Furthermore, it should be possible to represent the fact that one of the combustion chambers has burnt out (so that one of the engines is now different from the other three). The relational data model is not good at representing such structures. A richer data model is required, which is capable of capturing the fact that some chunks of data "belong" to other chunks, or that it only makes sense to have an item in the database if some other item is present (for example, you shouldn't store the temperature of a non-existent combustion chamber). This last requirement means that one should not only be able to define complex data structures, but also to enforce complex constraints on the existence of items. In fact, one should go further and be able to enforce constraints on the *behaviour* of items (temperatures outside a reasonable range should not be allowed, perhaps). It is also vital to store dependencies between items of data, and to act on them. For instance, if we use a new type of combustion chamber, the effects on the engine, and even on the whole aircraft, should be tracked.
The support of "Objects" in a DBMS is clearly one way of providing such capabilities. More generally, however, the support of "Semantic Data Models" is required, namely data models which can be tailored to the semantics of the application area.

There are other requirements; these are not satisfied automatically just because Objects or Semantic Data Models are supported, but they are easier to satisfy if this is so. It should be possible to issue arbitrarily complex queries: "What is the predicted fuel flow five seconds before the combustion chamber burns out?" Note that not only the formulation of such queries may be arbitrarily complex. Responding to them may require significant amounts of computation, since the required item of data may not have been computed previously (or may have been computed but not kept in the database).

It should also be possible to modify the "data schema"; in Object Oriented terms, this means it should be possible to modify the defined classes dynamically, without shutting down the DBMS. Although it is possible to define some classes which are clearly going to be useful for a particular application area, each project is likely to have special needs, either for new classes, or for modified classes (for instance adding new attributes to existing objects).

Finally, design engineers are constantly trying new things. This means that much of their use of any CAD system will be more akin to "programming" than to "database querying". It is very desirable to give them a "seamless" join of the two activities. Ideally, they should be able to use the same language whenever they communicate with the CAD system, no matter which type of task they are engaged on. Languages which are capable of providing such an interface have been called "Database Programming Languages".[2]

11.3 Special Case: Control System Design

Figure 11.1 shows a typical control engineering problem, in the form in which it may appear to the control engineer at some stage of design.[3] It shows the "pitch" control system for an aircraft. The figure is highly abstracted from mechanical or electrical components; each box shows a process, and the lines joining the boxes show quantities which are significant for the operation of the system. One group of boxes – labelled "Dryden wind gust model" – models the effect of turbulence on the aircraft. Another – "Short-period longitudinal..." – models the dynamic behaviour of the airframe. A third – "Controller" – represents some hardware/software combination which operates the aircraft's tail control surfaces; this is what has to be designed by the control engineer, and we see it with a design already proposed.

A typical task which the control engineer might undertake at this stage is to compute the normal acceleration experienced by the pilot when a sudden gust occurs, and to plot it as a graph against time. Another one might be to compute the RMS value of this acceleration when gusts occur randomly.

Figure 11.1 shows a dynamic system. But each of the groups of boxes to which we have referred can itself be viewed as a system, and even each individual box can be so viewed. Because of this, and because "systems" are central to the way in which control engineers think about things, we developed the data model shown in Figure 11.2 to support control engineering. This shows an entity "System" with five attributes, each of which may itself be an entity with attributes. For example, the "Definitions" attribute has a "Structure" attribute, which is used to define a system in terms of smaller systems, just as the system shown in Figure 11.1 is composed of boxes, which are themselves systems. (This shows that there is a need to support recursive data models, which can be used to represent instances of arbitrary complexity.) Some of the attributes in this data model are compact, well-structured entities. But attributes such as "Time response" are likely to consist of a substantial amount of data produced by some application program, and "Classification" may contain arbitrary strings.

We captured the data for this example using a top-down definition of the top-level system, with each of the three groups of boxes being defined as a system. Figure 11.3 shows the "Short-period longitudinal ..." box, as seen in a window of a graphical interface to our design environment. This box can be connected in place in the top-level system either before or after its internal structure has been defined.

11.4 How Object Oriented Should We Get?

Any Object Oriented system should support the notions of Objects, Object Identity (independent existence), Classes, and Inheritance.[2] Most proposals for "smart" DBMS systems can be considered to be "Object Oriented" by this criterion, even if one has to equate "object" with "entity", "class" with "type", and so on. But purists will insist on narrower definitions; in particular, that "objects" must be encapsulated, so that they can be accessed only by means of their own "methods".

Consider what this means for our control engineering example. The designer may be in the middle of some analysis; for example, simulating the behaviour of the aircraft in response to a command from the pilot. This may involve monitoring (querying) one or more of the variables which appear in Figure 11.1, such as the "tail surface deflection". During (or after) this simulation the designer may decide to rerun it with a different parameter value in one of the "controller" boxes. In order to arrive at an appropriate value, it may be necessary to examine some other attribute of the entire system, such as its "frequency response" (which is one of the attributes of the data model shown in Figure 11.2). Or the designer may need to consult the design specification, which may itself be stored as another instance of a "system", in order to see how satisfactory the current design is. The important phenomenon here is that the designer is accessing various entities (objects) throughout the database in a virtually random manner. In view of this, there seems little point in insisting on strict encapsulation.

The whole point of encapsulation is to impose restrictions on what can be accessed from where. In our application there should be no such restrictions. Strict encapsulation therefore imposes a burden, with-

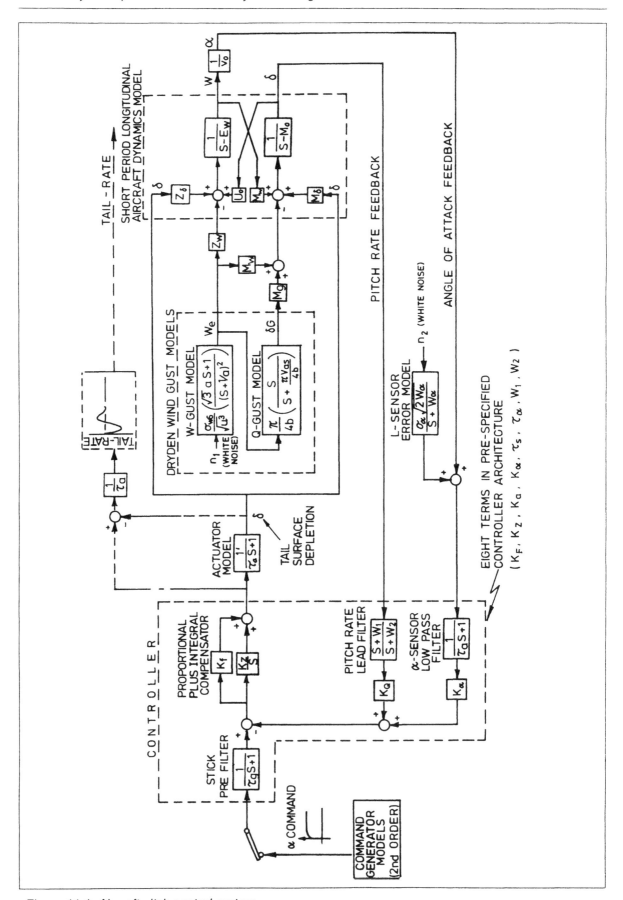

Figure 11.1: Aircraft pitch control system

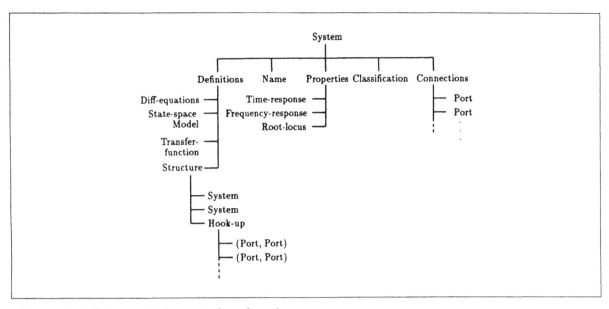

Figure 11.2: Data model for control engineering

out providing any benefits. Enforcing it would require the database programmer/user (often the same person in engineering design) to define and modify "methods" explicitly every time a new entity or attribute was defined, or an existing one modified. In practice it would lead to every class having a "get-attribute" and a "put-attribute" method which was inherited from the top-level class. This is exactly what seems to happen in some Object Oriented DBMS systems, but it appears to us to contravene the spirit of the Object Oriented approach – and for good reason, since strict "object-orientation" just gets in the way in cases like ours.

We make these remarks as an observation, rather than a dogmatic statement. There are no doubt applications, even in our own field, when encapsulation is beneficial. For example, in the process industries plant operators may wish to import models of individual processes from the suppliers of those processes. They will then derive all the usual advantages obtained when developing modular software if they specify the behaviour of those models in a strictly Object Oriented way. But the fact is that sooner or later their engineers will want to peek at what is going on inside the imported models. There appears to be a research problem here: how to assess the trade-off between the two ways of doing things, and how to allow both approaches to co-exist.

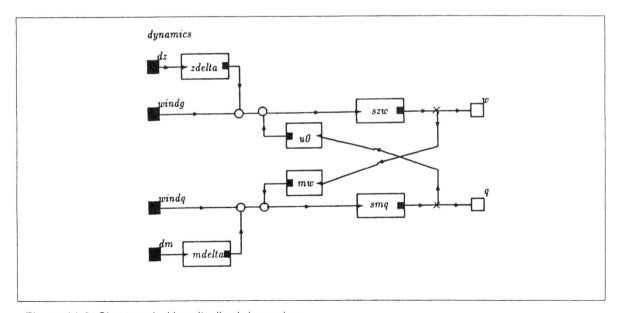

Figure 11.3: Short-period longitudinal dynamics

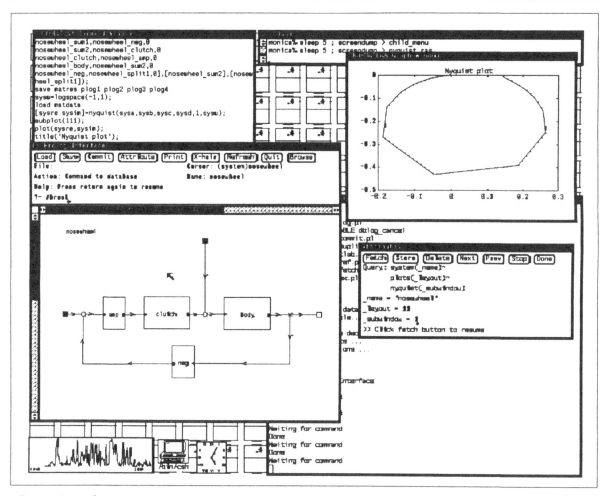

Figure 11.4: Computer console during DB-Prolog session

11.5 An Implementation Based on DB-Prolog

We have implemented a database programming environment to support control engineers engaged on design. We shall give only a very brief summary here; details can be found in Tan, C.Y., and Maciejowski, J.M., 'DB-Prolog: A database programming environment for CACSD'.[4] The implementation is based on extending Prolog with database-like facilities: persistence of data beyond one session, built-in integrity checking, update and querying facilities, data definition facilities. We have not provided important features such as support for long transactions or concurrent access by multiple users.

We have achieved a genuine "seamless" database programming language which handles data model definition, data instantiation, querying, and general "programming" (though the spirit of the environment is that one "programs" by issuing queries or making assertions). A semantic data model with classification, inheritance and aggregation is supported ("Objects without encapsulation", roughly), arbitrary computable constraints are allowed in data model definitions, and arbitrary computable queries may be issued. We call this language DB-Prolog. The data model is developed in "layers": a general-purpose layer inherent in DB-Prolog which defines a general semantic data model in terms of facts, attributes, constraints, rules and "is-a" relationships. There is then an application-level layer which defines entities appropriate to a particular application (e.g. "system" for control engineering). Finally there is the "population" layer which consists of specific instances of objects, associated with a particular design project.

A practical difficulty encountered by the user is that "navigating" around an object with a structure as complex as that shown in Figure 11.1 is quite awkward. A lengthy DB-Prolog predicate has to be constructed to access an attribute of a low-level box, for instance, if it is referred to by its place in the structure rather than by its name – for example, if one wishes to query "the frequency-response of the second box in the Dryden wind gust model". To overcome this we have developed a graphical interface which greatly simplifies the use of DB-Prolog when it is used for control engineering. This is tailored to the structure of the "system" entity, and a different interface would have to be developed for other applications.

Figure 11.4 shows the appearance of the computer screen during a DB-Prolog session with the graphical interface in use. (The example shown is not the same one as in Figure 11.1). A "system" entity is shown in the form of a block diagram, similar to Figure 11.1. To query an attribute of one of the blocks, the user "clicks" with the mouse on the block. A menu then appears by the block allowing the user to select further actions. If a query or update is selected a further pull-down menu opens listing the attributes of the block. This menu is changed dynamically if the data model changes. That is, if a new attribute is added to the "system" entity, the menu will contain the new attribute the next time it is pulled down. Updates to the database are performed using "form-filling" techniques, the "forms" also changing dynamically when required. It is of interest to note that implementation of the graphical interface was very easy and rapid; all the difficulty lay in the much earlier step of defining an appropriate data model for the application area.

Responding to certain queries, such as "How does the acceleration experienced by the pilot change with time when a wind gust is encountered?" requires considerable numerical computation (unless the same query has been made before, in which case the response is already stored in the database as a "fact" clause). The enforcement of certain constraints on data (e.g. "Only stable controllers are allowed") also requires such computation. In DB-Prolog this computation is performed by Matlab, which is proprietary software for matrix-based computation. Matlab, like much control engineering software, is intended for interactive use, and the interface between it and DB-Prolog is by means of a simple but effective "mail-box" facility. In Figure 11.4 a Matlab window can be seen, which allows the DB-Prolog user to monitor what Matlab is doing. The user does not issue Matlab commands directly, however. When necessary, DB-Prolog queries are translated into Matlab command sequences, which are then executed by Matlab; output from Matlab is intercepted and translated appropriately by DB-Prolog, and is also stored in the database. The curve shown in Figure 11.4 has been drawn by Matlab, and is part of the response to a DB-Prolog query. (The curve is in fact a frequency response locus drawn on the complex plane.) It appears in a separate "Matlab graphics" window.

It is not possible to load rules (methods?) for answering all possible queries into the DBMS. For instance, returning to our aircraft example, if the user wishes to evaluate the RMS acceleration experienced by the pilot, he has to formulate one or more rules for computing RMS values. Once this has been done, however, these rules remain available for future use, so if the next project involves computing the RMS variation in acid concentration in a drying tower in a chemical plant, the relevant rules are already there. If a new "RMS" attribute is added to the "system" data model (which can be done dynamically) then the user only has to query that attribute for the rules to be triggered. In this sense the DBMS accumulates "expertise" as it is used, so that DB-Prolog displays some features usually associated with expert systems. It would be easy to extend these features to add an "expert adviser" design capability.

11.6 Conclusion

The development of a "smart" database management system has enabled us to provide very powerful CAD facilities for control engineers. Similar facilities could be provided for design engineers working in other disciplines. The key to this has been the development of a data model rich enough to represent the application domain, and of a system powerful enough to handle this data model.

We have certainly made use of structured data types, of inheritance ("is-a" relationships), and of aggregation (entities with entities as attributes). Our system is therefore "Object Oriented" to a large degree, though not strictly so, since we do not have encapsulated objects accessible only via methods.

Our conclusion is that for applications such as ours it is essential to support semantic data models, but that one may not need to go all the way to being strictly Object Oriented. If we were starting today (rather than 1987), we would probably base our work on an existing Object Oriented DBMS. But this would be for our internal software engineering purposes; the facilities available to the user would be essentially the same as those provided by DB-Prolog.

References

[1]   Stonebreaker, M., 'Introduction to the Special Issue on database prototype systems', *IEEE Transactions on Knowledge and Data Engineering*, 2, 1, pp.1-3, 1990; Joseph, J.V., Thatte, S.M., Thompson, C.W., and Wells, D.L., 'Object Oriented databases: design and implementation', *Proceedings IEEE*, 79, 1, pp.42-64, 1991.

[2]   Atkinson, M.P., 'Types and persistence in database programming languages', *ACM Computing Surveys*, 19, 2, 1987.

[3]   Rimer, M., and Frederick, D.K., 'Solutions of the Grumann F-14 benchmark control problem', *IEEE Control Systems Magazine*, 7, 4, pp.36-40, 1987.

[4]   Tan, C.Y., and Maciejowski, J.M., 'DB-Prolog: A database programming environment for CACSD', *Proceedings IEEE CSS Workshop on Computer Aided Control System Design, Tampa, Florida*, 1989; Tan, C.Y., and Maciejowski, J.M., 'A logic programming based CACSD environment', *Technical Report CUED/F-INFENG/TR46, Cambridge University Engineering Dept*, 1990; Tan, C.Y., 'DBGI: A graphical interface to DB-Prolog for control systems design', *Technical Report CUED/F-INFENG/TR43, Cambridge University Engineering Dept*, 1990; Tan, C.Y., 'DB-Prolog: A database programming environment for computer-aided control systems design', *Ph.D Thesis*, Cambridge University, 1991.

OBJECTS IN THE OFFICE – THE BENEFITS FOR USERS OF NEWWAVE

Chris Marshall
Hewlett-Packard

12.1 Introduction

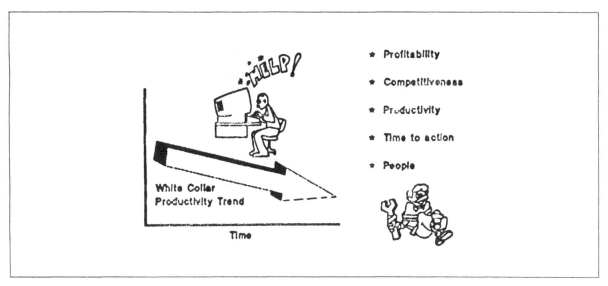

Figure 12.1: Challenges in the 1990s

In the last decade corporations discovered that the promise of increased productivity through computers has not happened. Companies are producing more reports, more paperwork, but their white collar workers are not producing as much real work. This has affected the corporation's bottom line making them:

* Less profitable

* Less competitive

* Less productive

and, more importantly, increasing the time it takes to make decisions and increasing the time it takes to act on decisions.

People in organisations have not been empowered by this flood of data on their PCs, they have been buried by it.

That's a very disturbing trend, especially since companies have been investing millions of dollars in computer hardware and software to try to increase white collar productivity. Why aren't these investments paying off? Of course, in some situations, computers are yielding measurable productivity gains. But why mot more often?

Today, software applications are a collection of dissimilar tools rather than components of an integrated solution. Even a simple reporting task can become a nightmare when you have to combine data from several very different applications – database, spreadsheet, graphics, word processor...

12.2 Application Environment Needs

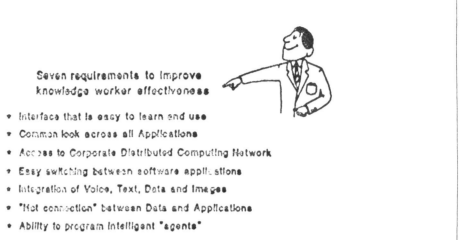

Figure 12.2: Application Environment Needs

Corporations have cried out to PC hardware and software vendors to deliver technologies that can help them reverse this white collar productivity trend.

In the later 1980s the US government sponsored a study on how PCs can be used in a more powerful way to improve productivity and profitability. John Young, HPs president, was on the panel. The panel came up with seven recommendations on how to increase the knowledge worker's productivity, using personal computers.

- Deliver an easy to use interface – no more C prompt!

- Give a common look and feel to PC SW.

- Give knowledge workers easy access to corporate networks – DBs on those networks.

- Allow for easy switching between tasks.

- Integrate new technologies – voice, communications, images, and data – not just text and number.

- Allow for "hot" or "live" connections between data and between tasks.

- Finally, let the computers do the work – through Agents, or system wide macros – to protect users from performing repetitive tasks.

These findings guided HP in developing NewWave.

12.3 What is NewWave?

One industry analyst said that "NewWave delivers the powers that PC manufacturers have been promising for the last five years."

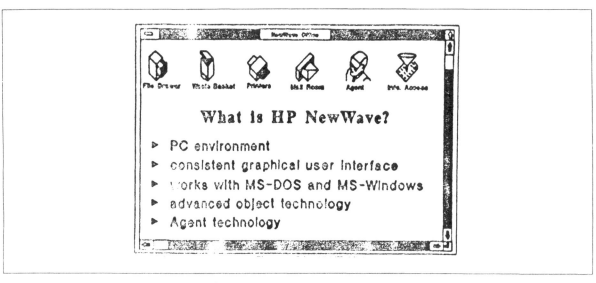

Figure 12.3: What is HP NewWave?

In short, you can explain HP NewWave as:

* a PC environment

* with a consistent G.U.I.

* built on standards DOS, Windows but going well beyond Windows with the true differentiators of

* advanced object technology

* and Agents/Task automation.

12.4 Benefits of NewWave

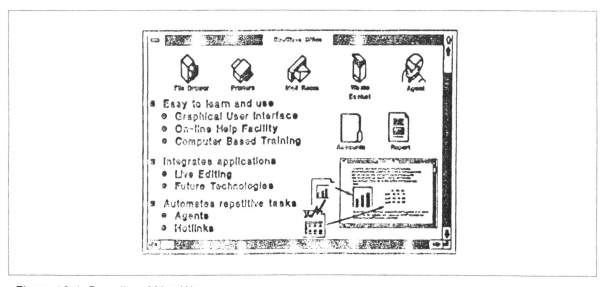

Figure 12.4: Benefits of NewWave

12.4.1 Ease of Use

The first thing you use is the G.U.I. Icons, pull-down menus, and a consistent look and feel across applications.

The natural, predictable user interface has been designed to be more like the physical world – an office metaphor. NewWave works the way you do.

The on-line help makes it easy to learn to use the full power of the system. CBT or computer based training is system wide, for NW, and NW applications. Corporate decision makers see NewWave as a way to have a consistent easy to learn and use environment for all their users.

12.4.2 Integrates Applications

NewWave is a lot more that just a pretty face, or G.U.I.

NewWave allows companies to integrate the data and applications on PCs so that users can use "drag and drop" actions to integrate say, a spread-sheet and a word processing document. NewWave then allows the spread-sheet to be edited with the document so giving the user live editing capabilities.

NewWave allows the integration of any application so providing a growth path for new and future technologies, such as video, voice and fax.

12.4.3 Automates Repetitive Tasks

Finally a real breakthrough we built into NewWave is the ability to "automate" repetitive tasks, enabling workers to turn these tasks back to the computer, for example, a manager in a company can automate the task of creating a monthly sales report.

* First, the agent would automatically download information from a database on a server, then update the text of the report, and finally the user would instruct the NewWave Agent, to send the report to a distribution list on the first Tuesday of every month.

NewWave also allows hotlinking, or true sharing of information/data throughout the system. Hotlinking is possible because of NW's object-based technology, which binds the data file and application EXE file together as one object.

OBJECT MANAGEMENT
The Implications

HIERARCHICAL OBJECT ORIENTED DESIGN

Peter J. Robinson
CANA Software Systems Limited

13.1 Introduction

This chapter gives an overview of HOOD. The *HOOD Reference Manual* Issue 3.0, produced by the European Space Agency in 1989, is currently the official definition of HOOD.

HOOD (Hierarchical Object Oriented Design) was developed by the European Space Agency as a design method for Ada, looking forward to the use of Ada as a major language for software for embedded space systems. It has now been taken up widely in large space systems such as Columbus, the European part of the International Space Station, Hermes, the manned space plane, and the new launch vehicle Ariane V. HOOD has also been adopted project wide for the European Fighter Aircraft, and is usually considered for any Ada software development projects because of its direct applicability and the availability of a range of HOOD Toolsets.

In the context of this publication, it should be pointed out that HOOD is primarily intended for software to be developed in Ada, but that IPSYS have recently developed a HOOD Toolset that has C++ as the corresponding implementation language. Therefore the Object Orientation of the design phase in HOOD is now being extended to the programming phase. In the context of databases, HOOD concentrates on the problem of identifying objects, but with more emphasis on procedural or processing aspects than on data structuring. However, neither aspect can or is treated in isolation.

The reader should therefore consider that this document defines HOOD as it is, and that HOOD is evolving to contribute to the design of systems that are Object Oriented both in terms of programming and of database techniques.

13.2 HOOD Method

13.2.1 HOOD Design Process Overview

The design strategy is globally top-down and consists of a set of basic design steps, in each of which a given object, called a parent object, is decomposed into a set of components called child objects which together provide the functionality of the parent object. This process of decomposition starts with the decomposition of the top level parent object called the root object which represents an abstract model of the system to design. Each component object in turn may be decomposed into other lower level objects in the following design steps until the bottom level or terminal object is reached. Terminal objects are designed in detail without further decomposition, i.e. the design provides for direct implementation into code.

A HOOD design can thus be modelled by a Design Process Tree (DPT), with several design levels, where upper-levels objects correspond to higher abstractions and/or functions whereas lower level objects are closer to programming abstractions.

Figure 13.1 gives an example of such a Design Process Tree (DPT). The figure shows the root object, representing the system to design, at the top level of the tree (i.e. with no parent object). The design process may follow the graph shown as follows:

Design level 1
step 1 produces objects obj_1 obj_2 obj_3

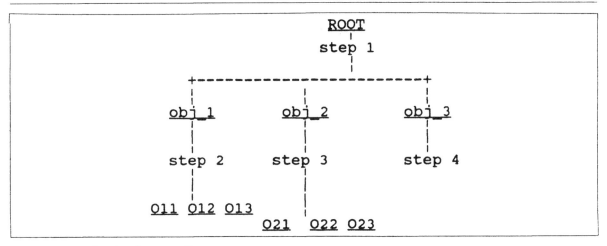

Figure 13.1: Design Process Tree

Design level 2
step 2 produces objects 011 012 013
step 3 produces objects 021 022 023
step 4 produces objects 031 ...

Design level 3
step 5, step 6, step 7 and so on.

Each object, except the root object, is completely defined through two successive design steps:

* **at level i-1:** an object is identified as a child object and partially specified through a first refinement of an ODS to specify its interfaces.

* **at level 1:** either the object is considered as a parent object and is decomposed into child objects, allowing a complete, validated, object description skeleton (ODS) to be produced, or the object is a terminal object and the details of the design are completed.

13.2.2 The Basic Design Step Overview

A basic design step has as goals the identification of child objects of a given parent object and of their individual relationships to other existing objects. This process is based on the identification of objects by means of OOD techniques which are described in section 13.3.

A basic design step process is further split into four phases, thus defining a micro life-cycle for a design step. The phases can be summarised as follows:

* **Problem definition.** The context of the object to be designed is stated, with the goal of organising and structuring the data from the requirement analysis phase. This is an opportunity to provide a completeness check on requirements and traceability to design.

* **Elaboration of an informal solution strategy**. The outline solution of the problem stated above is described in terms of objects at a high level of abstraction.

* **Formalisation of the strategy.** The objects and their associated operations are defined. A HOOD diagram of the proposed design solution is produced, allowing easy visualisation of the concepts and further formalisation.

* **Formalisation of the solution.** The solution is formalised through formal definition of provided object interfaces and formal description of object and operation control structures.

At the end of this phase, the design structure may be turned automatically into a Ada package and task structure from the ODS. Its usefulness and compilability depends on whether the content of the ODS conforms to Ada language.

13.2.3 The Basic Design Step (general scheme)

This overview may be expanded into a detailed description of the basic design step process as follows.

Phase 1: Problem definition

The description of the problem to be solved is split into two:

*   Statement of the problem. The designer states the problem in correct sentences which provide a clear and precise definition of the problem and the context of the system to design.

*   Analysis and Structuring of Requirement data. This sub-phase is the key point of the basic design step activities. The purpose of this analysis is to make sure that the problem has been well understood. Thus the designer gathers and analyses all the information relevant the problem including the environment of the system to design.

One way to proceed is to separate the requirements (already collected in the Software Requirement phase) into different types, mapped as follows:

*   static functional requirements used to identify objects and define the process to be done and may be reflected in the HOOD Operation Control Structures (OPCS).

*   dynamic functional requirements used to identify type of object; describe the dynamic behaviour of the system (when and under what conditions processing is to take place) may be specified in Petri Nets or State Transition Diagrams, and are incorporated in the Object Control Structures (OBCS).

*   non-functional requirements, which may be described in the ODS Implementation or Synchronisation Constraints.

If the requirement analysis work has already been done fully in an earlier phase of the software lifecycle, this analysis can be referenced in the relevant document, without repeating this work further in this HOOD step.

Phase 2: Elaboration of an informal solution strategy

The goal of this phase is to create an outline solution of the problem that has previously been defined. This outline solution is described by using a natural language, or a HOOD graphical representation explaining how the design is working for the current level of abstraction. The solution should describe the design by means of real world objects associated with the action which may be performed on them. This solution should not be considered as definitive, but as a baseline for further refinement in the following phase of the basic design step.

Phase 3: Formalisation of the strategy

This phase has as a goal the extraction of the major concepts of a solution strategy in order to come smoothly to a formalised description of the solution. If an informal description cannot be formalised, it may be because of the informal solution strategy is too incomplete; in this case it is recommended to go back to Phase 2.

*   Identification of objects. The designer identifies the objects by extracting nouns from the Informal Solution strategy. The designer must identify and structure these nouns according to their behaviour

and their associated level of abstraction (e.g. a noun may represent an object which is not relevant to the design at the current level of abstraction). The result of this phase is a textual description of each identified child object.

- Identification of operations. The designer identifies the operations by means of the same mechanism as in the previous sub-phase, but this time the verbs are extracted from the Informal Solution. All properties, related to the operation execution (i.e. parallelism, synchronisation, periodic execution), should also be reported in this phase. The result of this phase is a textual description of each identified operation.

- Grouping objects and operations. Each operation is then associated with an object. This grouping gives a structured representation of the strategy and helps establishing a formal description of the objects as well as completing a graphical description of the solution. The outcome of this phase is the list of the provided operations associated with each object. The previous two steps have separated the objects and the corresponding operations which were together in the Informal Strategy – this step simply regroups them in order to provide a clear definition for the next step.

- Graphic description. Using the HOOD graphical formalism, the designer produces a diagram corresponding to the solution outlined in the strategy with the child objects and operations identified above. This graphical representation should show the implemented_by links (for non-terminal object), the use relationship among objects, the dataflow and the exceptions. At this stage, object types will be also identified, either Active or Passive, Op_Control (to map parent operation to multiple child operations), Class Instance, Virtual_Node, or Environment object.

- Justification of design decisions. When a design decision is not obvious, or might not look obvious to a reviewer or maintainer in the future, the designer explains the reasons for his decision. In general, a justification is required to design those objects which are neither Passive nor Environment objects. In the same way, a justification is needed for each of those operations which are constrained.

The formalism of the strategy may lead to several iterations between itself and the elaboration of the solution strategy, until a sufficient understanding of the solution has been reached.

Phase 4: Formalisation of the solution

When the formalisation of the strategy has been completed, then the designer can elaborate a formal model of his solution, describing for a parent object the properties of each child object, the operations and the relationship among the child objects. This model is formally referred to as the Object Description Skeleton.

The capture of this formal description consists in filling each field of the Object Description Skeleton.

For each object, the Object Description Skeleton (ODS) contains:

- a formal description of the interfaces.

- a formal description of the Object Control Structure which provides the description of the synchronisation and relationships between constrained operations.

- a formal description of the Operation Control Structure for each provided or internal operation of the object.

- informal comments which may be added to describe the semantic behaviour, to provide useful information for further implementation or to justify possibly implementation decisions.

At the end of this phase, the ODS of the object is fully and formally described. From now on, it will remain the source of documentation for detailed design and code generation.

13.2.4 Basic Design Step Applied to the Robot Object

Unlike the other objects, the root object is completely defined through one basic design step. Thus the goals of the basic design step applying to the root object are:

• to define the interfaces of the root object;

• to identify its child objects and their relationships.

The impacts on the four phases of the basic design step are outlined hereafter:

Phase 1: Problem definition

The designer gathers and analysis all information relevant to the system to design with respect to the level of abstraction. Moreover the designer puts the emphasis on the environment of the System to Design (STD); he may produce or refer to a diagram showing the STD within its environment.

Phase 2: Elaboration of an informal strategy

This phase follows the general schemes.

Phase 3: Formalisation of the strategy

The process of identification of operations applied to the operations of the root object itself. Therefore the output of the sub-phase 'Grouping objects and operations' should also contain a list of associated provided operations for the root object. The graphical description should show:

• the root object and its operations;

• the relevant environment objects;

• the different child objects and their associated operations;

• all the use relationships, implemented_by link, the dataflow, exceptions...

Phase 4: Formalisation of the solution

All relevant fields of the Object Description Skeleton are filled in the way described in 'Graphical description'.

13.2.5 Basic Design Step Applied to Terminal Object

The basic design step applied to the terminal objects is shorter and each phase is restricted as follows:

Phase 1: Problem definition

The designer should gather all the information related to the terminal object.

Phase 2: Elaboration of an informal strategy

The purpose of this phase is to provide a description of the terminal object in order to be able to define the OBCS and OPCS(s) of the object, derived from the object identification of the Parent object. The goal defined in the general scheme of creating a solution strategy is not applicable here, as the terminal object is not decomposed any more.

Phase 3: Formalisation of the strategy

Not applicable.

Phase 4: Formalisation of the solution

This phase follows the general scheme define in 'Graphical description'.

OBJECT REUSABILITY: THE MAKING OF DATA MANAGEMENT

Malcolm Fowles
DCE Information Management Consultancy Ltd

14.1 Introduction

This chapter contends that the reusability of Object Oriented components makes them very amenable to being shared in a co-ordinated way across systems and other products of software development. It contrasts with the limited scope for sharing the components of current technology. Object Orientation is thus seen to push back the limitations on the successful management of shared resources, and hence to be the making of data management.

14.2 Information Resource Management

Data Management is a familiar example of a more general approach called Information Resource Management (IRM). IRM manages information resources for use in information products that meet business needs. It emphasises the building and maintenance of reusable assets, planned and co-ordinated under one point of responsibility.

Such asset management approaches are common in advanced industries. The role of assets is to reduce the time and cost in responding to new requirements and to increase the quality and consistency of the response. In IRM's case, this means, for example, the rapid exploitation of new business opportunities and the earlier provision of new information, a better business orientation of new systems, easier assessment and control of changes, less fragmentation and incompatibility between systems, less uncontrolled duplication and better integration of external information.

Data management based on conventional technology manages two types of asset, one logical and the other physical. The first, Data Administration, manages business data definitions, organised into assets according to the conventions of prevailing data analysis techniques. We might call this resource a co-ordinated view of information requirements. Whereas Database Administration manages the design and contents of an organisation's databases according to the dictates of the DBMS in use. This resource is the current information capability.

Process management (as opposed to data management) has never become a successful IRM function because a process definition in inherently unreusable. We shall return to this later. Only certain restricted types of code-level processes, such as sub-routines in a dynamic load library, are truly shareable.

14.3 Object Reusability

The reusability of objects comes from three mutually reinforcing features of object orientation. (Not all present day Object Oriented techniques or tools employ every aspect of them, and to that extent can deliver only part of the potential benefit.)

• Object encapsulate "processing" in the same module as the "data" it affects. Although the basic substance remains the same, encapsulation involves a completely different organisation of the elements from which systems are composed, one that is closer to the way we perceive the world. A different terminology is used, so we speak of object "behaviour" and "properties" as approximately the same features as process and data.

• Encapsulation weaves traditional aspects of good reusable modular design, namely high cohesion, low coupling and information hiding, into the very fabric of systems. An object collects all we know about a thing observed, what it can tell us and what we can do to it. A system is just a configuration of objects passing messages to each other.

- Objects can be classified, for example, in the way we say that a bird is a type of animal and also a type of flyer. This "is a type of" organisation is called Inheritance, because the descendant object (bird) inherits all the features, i.e. the properties and behaviour, of its ancestor objects (animal and flyer). Its own special features make it what it is.

- Classification makes it possible to eliminate all redundant definition, so that we never need to define a feature twice. Furthermore, objects can develop by difference or evolution. If a standard object does not exactly fit new circumstances or a particular business view, only the differences need be defined in a specialised type of the original, which is still used in so far as it is correct.

- Object behaviour and the restrictions upon it are more naturally specified by Rules than by the conventional idea of processing. Rules guarantee the correctness of an object's interface, thus turning it into a black box. This in turn makes an object reusable by anyone other than its implementer, by removing the need to understand how it works.

It is now possible to discuss the relative unreusability of processes. Their definition includes accesses to data which lies outside the module structure. The process is meaningless outside this context. It also has side effects on other processes through the data. Variations (by far the commonest type of reuse) can only be produced by duplicating and changing an original. And because of the data accesses we need to know how a process works as well as its interface, before we can reuse it.

14.4 Impacts of Object Orientation

14.4.1 General Benefits of Reuse

Data management pursues the same benefits of reuse, albeit restricted to the data side, as does object orientation. Productivity, quality, flexibility and responsiveness all follow from the reuse of assets as night follows day. However, the extent to which they do so depends on several factors, which are considered in turn.

Obviously it costs less to reuse an asset rather than build a component from scratch. But how much? There is a substantial difference between the costs of Object Oriented and conventional reuse. In the latter, copying and changing components or templates are the order of the day. Whereas the ability to specialise types of object without altering or copying originals means that a very high level of reuse can be achieved at a minimum cost of revalidation and subsequent maintenance.

How much more does it cost to design and make reusable assets rather than one-off components? The relative overhead to create reusable objects is lower in terms of achieving equivalent levels of reusability and replication. However, it may well increase in practice when we add the effort to reach the much higher levels now possible and the costs of managing many more assets than before.

Productivity increases with the number of occasions on which assets are reused. This is not affected by the technology itself, only by how it is managed. We shall return to this later.

Most benefit comes from the level of reuse, that is how much of a new product is composed of reused assets rather than changed or new components. Encapsulation of behaviour and rules massively increases the potential level of reused components in a new system. Data aspects make up about 10% of our systems and our development effort. Reusing data definition alone thus has a relatively minor impact on overall productivity and quality when compared with the 85% reuse that has been achieved by some users of object technology.

Better module cohesion and coupling combined with the ability to change by specialisation reduce the impact of change on systems configured from objects. This effect is usually the first thing mentioned by an Object Oriented developer, and seems to be easier to achieve than reusability. It is a major influence on flexibility and responsiveness to change.

14.4.2 Effects on the IRM Approach

Object Orientation is an enabling technology. It pushes back limits on what can be shared, on the ease of making assets reusable, and on actually reusing them. It also makes easier the management of change.

Encapsulation's effects on IRM are dramatic. Definition of properties, behaviour and rules are managed together. Where before we could only coordinate terminology, now we can include meaning. Since data definition makes up only a small proportion of a system (about 10%), the addition of behaviour and rules massively increases the scope for reusable assets.

Classification's effects are equally dramatic. If we took full advantage of the opportunity to eliminate redundancy, an organisation's systems would contain not a single duplicated line of code. Where parts of the business need different views of information (a great problem of data management), what is truly the same or must be standard can be coordinated in a shared object, isolating the differences in sub-types.

The introduction of rules has more subtle effects. Business rules themselves can be managed assets when they are expressed as rules of information objects. So can business objectives, since it is possible to formalise them as rules that *should* be true (rather than *must* be true). By feedback from business rules and objectives to the information model itself, IRM is able to tie information resources closer to business needs.

A massive increase in shareable information resources enables the use of a faster production system than we now employ, based on component assembly. The inclusion of more tested, standard and guaranteed information resources gives higher quality information products. The prior availability of such resources, their ease of adaptation and the smaller impact of change on them gives greater flexibility and response to the business.

14.5 Success Factors

14.5.1 Effective Management

Object Orientation may give us inherently more shareable resources than conventional technology, but it does not give automatic benefits. Actual reuse must be managed. Objects have to be acquired, stored, inventoried and more accessible, and distributed for assembly. Most important, they have to be planned. Planning the objects implies planning the scope of the products to be assembled from them, which is as much a responsibility of business planning or marketing as any other function.

There are two critical aspects of this planning. The first is to make sure that you will get sufficient use of the shared resources to pay back any extra effort to put in to acquire them. This means working out the number, frequency and form of future information products with common characteristics. It also means creating an incentive to use shared resources rather than build new components. The lack of any such incentive for conventional projects, other than the policing of standards, is one of the great problems of data management. By contrast, it is cheaper and easier to reuse objects because of their ease of change and extension.

The second critical success factor is to plan the right assets in the first place. Then the number of times assets are used, the level of reuse in each product, and the extent of future changes will all be improved. On the management side, this implies taking a viewpoint above individual projects, at the level of a group of products with common characteristics. One example is a business area which will use the same business objects in several systems, and in such a case both object and data management have the same goal. However, there are other ways to define common product characteristics, such as a shared user interface standard, and good management must find which ways deliver the most benefit.

14.5.2 Effective Techniques

Experience says it is possible, indeed easy, to create a system composed of objects that are unusable elsewhere. So, for a set of components to be effectively reusable in many systems it must be not only conceived but also designed for the purpose.

Objected Oriented business analysis techniques identify objects, their behaviour and the rules which govern them. They are not too dissimilar to conventional analysis techniques, it is just that the final results are organised into objects rather than into separate data and (unreusable) process models. The techniques have to be able to analyse a group of products if necessary, and here the use of rules to model business objectives comes into its own. Objectives are, as it were, the business equivalent to the requirements specification of an individual system.

Object Oriented design techniques identify a physical implementation which optimises costs given the available technology, and are more varied because the technology is more varied.

Analysis and design take just as long as before if there are no components to reuse. There is the same need for good people to carry them out. Indeed, it makes sense to use the best people and to spend more on refinement for shared resources than for a single system. If over half of all new developments will be composed of shared resources, responsibility for resource management must rise to the top. Object management should be treated as the flagship of an IT department, and will ultimately be its controlling function.

14.6 Conclusion

Other industries making the transition to asset management have halved their costs, improved their construction time dramatically, turned estimating and scheduling into reliable disciplines, and begun true marketing. The potential of treating information resources as assets is huge.

We can now see that data management is the right idea fighting with the wrong technology. Technical factors limit what is economically reusable. Object Orientation pushes these limits right back. The control of unreusable processes by individual projects has made data management a political and technical struggle against enormous odds, and it has only succeeded where there has been absolute management commitment. The encapsulation of processing in objects and its effect on the economic case for reuse swings the balance the other way.

To succeed, some very basic changes in outlook are necessary. For example, we need to forecast demand for the right resources as much as react to demand for individual information products. And hence we need techniques (such as objectives analysis) which focus on future demand as well as current requirements.

Perhaps the most fundamental change is the switch from a linear, one-off software production system in which data management is a struggling support function to an iterative, continuous product development function controlled by resource planners and managers. Software practitioners are still wearing blinkers, and discuss Object Oriented analysis, design and construction as if they are replacement techniques for the stages of its life-cycle. Data management is well placed to take a wider view, and is thus the most appropriate function to introduce its business to the benefits of Object Orientation. In return, as an enabling technology, Object Orientation will be the making of data management.

OBJECT DATABASE DESIGN

Colette Rolland and Joel Brunet
University of Paris

15.1 Introduction

Conventional conceptual models do not fit well with the promising Object Oriented databases systems. In this chapter we present an Object Oriented conceptual model which combines the assets of the conventional semantic models with the advantages of the Object Oriented approach. We propose methodological guide-lines for helping the analyst in the selection of candidate objects, the identification of the pertinent ones, their structure and their classification in the inheritance hierarchy.

In recent years there has been a substantial influence of Object Oriented programming languages on the Database Management System (DBMS) technology. This has resulted in the development of a number of Object Oriented data models and system.[1] An Object Oriented modelling method offers a number of important advantages, such as:

- uniformly (all information is modelled through the same concept, namely object).

- encapsulation that packs the structure and behaviour of an object together.

- classification which allows to define abstract data types.

- inheritance through which classes are organised into a hierarchy.

- overloading and overriding.

- composition of objects (an object can contain another object).

On the other hand, conceptual models have been proved to be extremely useful in the early stages of information system development in order to translate the users requirements into a supposedly precise, complete and unambiguous description, the so called conceptual schema. Advantages of conceptual modelling are:

- high level specification (the conceptual schema is a real-world model that only deals with conceptual issues).

- abstraction of representation of implementation details (the specifier can concentrate on the problems, the "whats" of requirements specification, taking away the "hows" of technical design).

- readability and communicability (the conceptual schema serves as a tool to communicate with the users' community and to validate the specification).

- semantic power of concepts that allow a precise characterisation of entity types, their associations and the integrity constraints.

- integration of structure and behaviour (earliest conceptual models have focussed on data modelling with the purpose to facilitate the interpretation of data semantics and to allow the description of the database contents in high level conceptual terms). Nowadays it has been clearly demonstrated that a conceptual schema must incorporate construction to deal with both static and dynamic properties and rules of the information system.

Well known examples of conceptual models are Entity-Relationship models,[2] Binary Relationship models,[3] Functional model,[4] Event based models,[5] Semantic models.[6]

Until now there is no clear connection of a conceptual schema to an Object Oriented system. It may be even questioned if such a connection is opportune or necessary. Some people may argue that Object Oriented data models make conceptual models completely redundant.

It is our opinion that even in an OODBMS environment, a conceptual modelling is still desirable. Conceptual modelling has the purpose of abstracting and conceptualising relevant parts of the application domain. It allows one to build in a conceptual schema that serves as a specification reference by giving an unambiguous description of the conceptual issues of the system which can be understood by non-technical persons.

In addition, it is the authors' belief that the entire analysis and design process should be based on the Object Oriented approach. This will avoid the modelling paradigms mismatch providing a unifying approach that would facilitate iteration and emphasis on reuse.

Thus, the conceptual schema of the Object Oriented database application should be Object Oriented itself.

The chapter aims at presenting a conceptual Object Oriented model, namely O*, which combines the assets of conventional conceptual models and the advantages of the Object Oriented approach. The step from an Object Oriented conceptual schema to an Object Oriented implementation will then be much easier and the full power of the Object Oriented approach can then be exploited.

The chapter is organised as follows. In section 15.2 we describe the O* model. Section 15.3 emphasises the semantics of conceptual objects. Finally, we introduce in section 15.4 methodological guidelines for helping the analyst in building in the conceptual schema.

15.2 The O* model

15.2.1 The Object Concept

An object is a conception of a persistent phenomenon of the application domain, which contains relevant information for the future database application. For example, in a customer's application, phenomena like a *specific client* or a *specific order* will be regarded as objects whereas an *order-arrival* or a date will not be (the first one is an instantaneous event and the second one is a property which is significant only in the context of an object).

An object may be considered at two levels: the type level and the instance level. At the type level an object belongs to a class; its definition is an object scheme which describes the structure, the behaviour and the dependency links for all objects of the same class. At the instance level an object has a state which evolves over the time when events occur; its definition is an object life-cycle which describes why and how the state of an object is affected. An object has its own identity which allows it to be differentiated from other objects.

Finally, an object is a triplet $o = (Sch, G, Id)$ where *Sch is the object scheme, G is the object life-cycle and Id its identification.* The three components of the object definition are described in turn.

Object scheme

The scheme of an object o is an abstract description of the form

Sch(o) = (Pro, Ope, Cns, Ref, Evt), where

- Pro refers to the set of properties of the object.

- Ope refers to the set of possible operations on the object.

- Cns describes the constraints to be verified by the object.

- Ref refers to the static links of the object with other objects. It consists of a set of references.

- Evt refers to the set of events which may be stimulated by particular state changes of the object.

The first three items Pro, Ope and Cns, characterise the local aspects of the object, while Ref and Evt specify the context of the object, i.e. its interactions with the other objects. All these items are presented in sections 15.2.2 to 15.2.6. The object schemes are organised into an inheritance hierarchy, which is detailed in section 15.2.7.

An object scheme may be viewed as a matrix which specifies the structure and the behaviour of a population of objects, namely the scheme instances. The set of the instances of a scheme A, at a given time, is called the extension of the scheme and is denoted Ext(A).

Identity

Each object has an unique identifier. The major consequence is that objects have an existence independent of their state. This well known concept in Object Oriented systems,[7] must be kept in mind during the conceptual modelling. Thus, the notion of scheme extension may be more precisely defined as the set of identifier values of the scheme instances.

State change and life-cycle

The state of an object is defined as the concatenation of all its properties and references values at a given time. A state change of an object is due to the triggering of an operation by an event. The change results of the operation execution.

The set of all its state changes characterises the life-cycle of the object. The life-cycle may thus, be defined as the set of events which trigger these state changes. For an object o, the life-cycle is denoted $G(o) = \{Ev_i(o)\}$ where $i=0..n$. $G(o)$ is bounded by:

- the event Ev_0 corresponding to the birth of o, and

- the event Ev_n corresponding to the death of o.

For instance, the life-cycles of the two order o and o' may be respectively $G(o)$ = {order arrival, order delivery, order invoicing} and $G(o')$ = {order arrival, order cancellation}.

Events are totally ordered according to time. We denote: $Ev_i \leq Ev_j$ if Ev_i occurs before or at the same time as Ev_j. Inclusion of life-cycles is defined as follows:

$$\Gamma(o') \subseteq \Gamma(o) \leftrightarrow Ev_0(o') \geq Ev_0(o) \text{ and } Ev_n(o') \leq Ev_n(o)$$

We will see later on that the life-cycle notion plays an important role in the construction of object schemes. This definition is different from the Object life-cycle definition of A. Sernadas *et al*,[8] for whom the object life-cycle is the sequence of permitted events for a given object.

15.2.2 Properties

An object is composed of properties which determine its structure. Properties are "part of" the object

---

(a)

object CLIENT
properties
      account : { number : INTEGER
               amount : DECIMAL }
      address : STRING

(b)

object CLIENT
properties
      account : ACCOUNT
      address : STRING

(c)

object ORDER
properties
      lines : Set_of (ORDER-LINE)

Figure 15.1: Objects and their Properties

definition. For example, in Figure 15.1a, *Address* and *Account* are part of the *Client* scheme. A property is strongly dependent of the owner object, and determines one of its measurable characteristics. A property may be changed only by the operations defined in the object scheme. A property is defined by a name and a set of values. It may take its values either in a domain or in a scheme extension.

Domains are either predefined (INTEGER, STRING...) or user-defined by enumeration and aggregation. In Figure 15.1a, *Account* is a complex domain defined by a *number* (which is an INTEGER) and an *amount* (which is DECIMAL). The fact that a property value belongs to a scheme extension means that we allow that an object (namely the aggregate object) can contain another object (namely the component object). In Figure 15.1b, *Account* is an object defined by an object scheme elsewhere. The two alternatives are correct and their choice depends on the analyst. The link between the object and one of its properties is called the composition link. It can be simple or multiple. Figures 15.1a and 15.1b illustrate simple composition while Figure 1c illustrates multiple composition. The composition link, between an aggregate object and its component objects, must satisfy the following constraint:

a scheme A is composed of a scheme B if

$$\forall o \in A: \exists o_1 \in B / Ev_0(o_1) = Ev_0(o)$$
$$\exists o_2 \in B / Ev_n(o_2) = Ev_n(o)$$
$$\forall o' \in comp(o), \Gamma(o') \subseteq \Gamma(o)$$

where the function comp returns the set of instance o' which have been components of o during its life-cycle.

This means that the behaviour of component objects is strongly coupled to the behaviour of their aggregate object. For example, in Figure 15.1b, any creation of a *client* instance implies the creation of its *account* and similarly, the deletion of any *client* instance implies the deletion of its *account*. In this case, the life-cycle inclusion property is satisfied because an account always depends on a client and cannot be transferred to another client. The multiple composition link follows the same rule: *orders* (Figure 15.1c) are always created with at least one *order-line*, and when they are deleted all *lines* are deleted too.

15.2.3 Operations

Object changes are due to the execution of operations. Following the encapsulation principle, we assume that an object may be altered only by the means of one of its operations. An operation has a name and a text specifying the rule according to which properties and references are valued and changed.

15.2.4 Constraints

Static constraints on objects, i.e. constraints which are independent of time, must be taken into account in the conceptual schema. Some kind of static constraints, which concern relationships between two objects (e.g. referential constraints, cardinality constraints) are specified by instanciation of the composition and reference concepts. Other static constraints are local to an object and may be expressed by natural language sentences or by equations on the scheme properties and references. They are specified in the constraint item of the object scheme, as illustrated in Figure 15.3.

The Eiffel model uses the similar concept of class invariant.[9] In the Oblog model,[10] a first order temporal language captures both static and dynamic constraints on the object attributes. In the O* model, the dynamic constraints are represented by means of operations and events.

15.2.5 References

The reference link specifies a static relationship between two objects. It allows that an object scheme uses the services of another object scheme. This means that the referred scheme instances will be shared by the referring schemes instances.

References are simple or multiple. For instance, in Figure 15.2, the object *Order* refers to only one *client* (simple reference) but to several *products* (multiple reference).

In addition, the referring relationship must satisfy the following constraint: a scheme A refers to a scheme B if

$$\exists o' \epsilon B / \forall o \epsilon A / ref(o) = o'$$
$$Ev_0(o) \neq Ev_0(o') \text{ or } Ev_n(o) \neq Ev_n(o')$$
$$\forall o \epsilon A, \Gamma(o) \subseteq \Gamma(ref(o))$$

where the function ref returns the set of instances o' which have been referred by o during its life-cycle.

An *order* refers to a *client* who may be shared by several *orders* (Figure 15.2). The reference constraint expresses that a *client* may be created (or deleted) without any referring *orders*; but the life-cycle of an *order* is included into the life-cycle of its corresponding *client*. The same considerations are true for the multiple reference between *order* and *product*.

15.2.6 Events

The event concept[11] is introduced in order to model the dynamic aspects of the application domain. Operations express how objects change. Events explain why they undergo changes. An event occurs when a noteworthy state change happens either in the environment or on one object of the database. It

```
        object   Order
        references
            c : Client
            ps : Set_of ( PRODUCT )
```

Figure 15. 2: Object and References

triggers one or several operations on one or several objects. An event stimulated by the environment is referred to as an external event while an event due to an object state change is called internal event.

An event has a name. Its definition includes a predicate part which specifies its occurrence conditions, and a triggering part which specifies the operations to be triggered with their associated conditions and iterations. For example (in Figure 15.5), an *order arrival* is an external event that triggers the insertion of a new *Order*, the conditional creation of a new *client* and its associated *account* (if the order refers to a new client). In the same figure, the *out of stock* event is an internal event activated by the object *Stock* when the quantity in stock becomes lower than the replenishment level. The *out of stock* event triggers the *supply* operation on *Supplier*.

15.2.7 Inheritance

Objects are organised into inheritance hierarchies. We says that a scheme S is a specialisation of a generic scheme G if the two following properties are verified.

• the scheme inclusion property: $G \subseteq S$

This expresses that the scheme of S inherits the properties, operations, constraints, references and events defined in the scheme of G.

• the extension inclusion property: $Ext(G) \subseteq Ext(S)$

For each instance of the specialised scheme there is a corresponding instance with the same identifier value in the generic scheme. This implies that at the instance level, identifier values of the generic scheme instances are inherited by the specialised scheme instances. An identifier value may be inherited by several instances of different specialised schemes. This important feature of our inheritance notion expresses that an entity of the real world may be described in more than one scheme instance. Sciore calls the set of specialised instances of a generic scheme instance *independent perspectives* of the entity.[12] Each perspective represents a role of the entity in a determined context. Disjoint and inclusion constraints between the instances of specialised objects may be specified in the constraints part of the generic scheme.

Operations may be redefined in a specialised scheme. A specialised operation is triggered off in addition to the generic operation, in accordance with the augmentation principle.[13] Events may also be redefined.[14] This allows to trigger additional operations for a specialised object. The event predicate may be overridden.

15.2.8 Scheme Representations

A textual description of object schemes as well as different diagrammatic representations are associated to the O* model. Figure 15.3 shows the textual description of the objects *Order* and *Product*. Two kinds of graphs allow the visualisation of the static interrelations (Figure 15.4) and dynamic interrelations (Figure 15.5).

15.3 Object Semantics

O* implies a typology of objects in which each kind of objects has its own semantics. The typology results of both static links and dynamic links.

15.3.1 Static Links

Objects can relate one to another in three different ways: by composition, by referring and through inheritance hierarchies. Composition and referring links allow us to structure objects while inheritance is a mean for classifying objects.

```
object  ORDER
      properties
            name : STRING
            lines : SET_OF ( ORDER-LINE )
            creation_date : DATE
            delivery_date : DATE
            invoice_date : DATE
            cancellation_date : DATE
            state : [created, delivered, invoiced]
      operations
      creation :%order creation and order lines insertion %
      delivery :%change of order state after delivery%
      invoice :%change of order state after invoicing%
      cancellation : % order  and related order lines deletion%
      constraints
            creation_date < delivery_date
            creation_date < invoice_date
            delivery_date < invoice_date
      references
            c : Client
object  PRODUCT
      properties
            name : STRING
            quantity : INTEGER
            replenishment_level : INTEGER
      operations
      creation: % augmentation of stock%
      taking out: %diminution of stock%
      events
            out of stock :predicate
                  Old.quantity >= replenishment_level
                  New.quantity < replenishment_level
            triggers
                  supply on Supplier
```

Figure 15.3: Textual Description of Objects

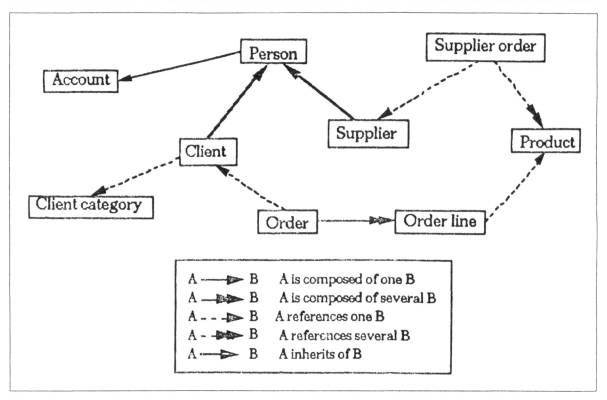

Figure 15.4: Static Interrelations

According to the composition link, objects can be classified into *simple objects* and *composite objects*. Objects which are only composed of domain-based properties are called simple objects; conversely a composite object contains one (simple composition) or several (multiple composition) objects. For example, the object *client* in Figure 15.1a is a simple object while in Figure 15.1b it is a composite object. Simple objects have a tuple-like structure while composite objects have a hierarchical one. Composition expresses structural links among objects whose behaviour is strongly coupled: the under- lying semantics of composition is that the life-cycles of component objects is totally embedded in the

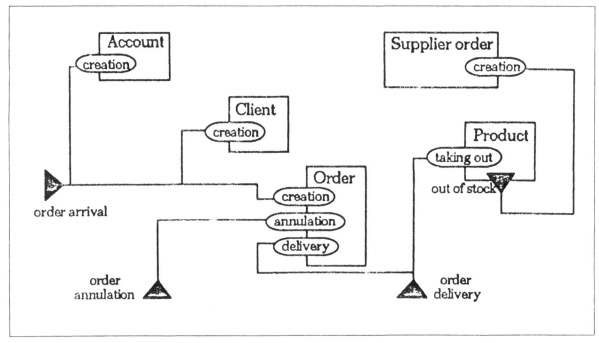

Figure 15.5: Dynamic Interrelations

```
object  ASSIGNMENT
references
        e : EMPLOYEE with role INVOLVED-EMPLOYEE
        p : PROJECT with role AFFECTED-EMPLOYEE
```

Figure 15.6: Associative Objects

aggregate object life-cycle. This helps the analyst to make the distinction between independent objects (whose life depends only from themselves) and embedded objects depending of other objects.

Referring links express transient relationships among objects. They allow us to make the distinction between *associative objects* and *object roles*. Associative objects are those which refer to other objects. The life-cycle of such objects is shorter than the life-cycle of the referred objects. Semantically an associative object may be viewed as a temporal relationship between objects that play within this relationship a specific role.

For instance, the object *Assignment* in Figure 15.6 refers to the object *Employee* (which plays the role of *Project-involved employee*) and the object *Project* (which plays the role of *affected project*). The *assignment* life-cycle corresponds to the duration of the involvement of employees within projects. It starts when the first employee is involved in a given project and ends when there are no more employees involved in projects.

An associative object uses the services (property access, operation inferring...) of the referred objects. In essence simple and composite objects are stable objects while associative objects are more volatile ones which describe temporal roles of stable objects.[15] The O* definition of the composition and the referring links helps the analyst making the distinction between them.

The inheritance link is a mean of object schemes factorisation through the specialisation and the generalisation mechanisms. It allows us to distinguish *specialised objects* from *generic objects*.

15.3.2 Dynamic Links

Dynamic relationships among objects are explicitly specified through events and operations triggering. We claim that it is important to make explicit these relationships at the conceptual step (instead of hiding them in the method code) because an important part of the real world complexity is due to these dynamic interactions.

While an operation is local to an object and simply gives a possible way of changing the object state, an event characterises two forms of dynamic interaction between two or several objects. Firstly, by grouping the set of operations to be triggered when a particular situation occurs, an event expresses synchronisation of operations upon objects. For instance, in Figure 15.5 the operation *taking out* on *product* is simultaneous to the operation *delivery* on *order*. Secondly, as operations may induce state changes that are in turn events, the events succedence makes clear the cascade of the objects transformations due to an initial signal. For instance, in Figure 15.5 the external event *order delivery* may induce the internal event *out of stock* which triggers a supply operation on the supplier object. Dynamic relationships allow us to separate *change objects* (they activate events and generate changes on other objects) and *state objects* (they store the state of real entities). In Figure 15.5 *Product* is a change object while *Client* is a state object.

The advantages of the event concept in the object definition are as follows:

* all the static and dynamic properties are specified into the object schemes. Object encapsulation is realised by operations and events.

- behavioural and operational dependencies are clearly specified.

- events lead us to study local situations fully delimited by a state change of only one object.

- events lead us to define at the conceptual step of system development the semantics of the message calls modifying the information system, which otherwise is defined only at the design level into the methods scripts.

Our notion of event is similar to the rule concept of Tsalgatidou and Loucopoulos,[16] except that there is one rule per operation while there are several operations triggered by an event. Petri nets diagrams[17] have not been retained because of their expensive representation cost.

15.4 Methodological Guide-lines

15.4.1 Overview

This section is an overview of the methodological guide-lines that may be followed by the analyst to reach the object schemes specification. We identify four basic steps:

- inventory of initial objects.

- identification of final objects.

- identification of operations.

- identification of events.

These steps are performed iteratively. The number of iterations will depend on how deeply the analyst chooses to perform the tasks related to each step for a given iteration.

15.4.2 Inventory of Initial Objects

The identification of the object schemes starts with the analysis of the application domain entities, in association with a search of reusable pre-existing objects. Three kinds of real entities may be identified: *physical things, actors and entity relationships.* For instance, a product is a physical things, a client is an actor, and an order associates various entities. These three kinds of entities may be represented as objects. The inventory of relevant actors, physical things and relationships serves at the basis for identifying initial objects and defining them through object schemes.

15.4.3 Identification of Final Objects

Thus, with a first population of object schemes, the following rules are used to infer complementary schemes, in order to be nearing the completeness of the specification.

- compare object life-cycles: this may lead to object explosion, object grouping or introduction of new objects.

- if the life-cycle of a component object is distinct from the life-cycle of its composite object, thus the composite object must be split into two or more independent objects; assume that the analyst perceived the *client* as part of the definition of the *order* object, the rule will help him to separate *Client* and *Order*.

- if two objects have exactly the same life-cycle they must be aggregated to form a composite object: starting with two different objects *Hotel* and *Room*, the rule may suggest to embed *rooms* in *hotels*.

- the intersection of life-cycles of two related objects may suggest the introduction of an associative object whose life-cycle is included in both object life-cycles. Let's assume that the objects *Product* and *Client* have been initially identified. The life-cycle of a client may be larger than the life-cycle of a product and vice versa. The intersection of their life-cycle highlights an associative object which is the *order* object.

- examine multiple referring. This may result in the introduction of new objects: a multiple reference may be broken in order to take into account a new object scheme, if its characterisation is useful. For example, the object scheme *Order line* may therefore be characterised between *Order* and *Product*.

- use generalisation and specialisation abstractions. Generalisation and specialisation mechanism may point out some object schemes, respectively by factorisation and specialisation of scheme contents.

- study the variability of references. In order to keep track of the fact that references are changing over time, it can be necessary to introduce an historical object scheme. For instance, a *client* may change of *category*. An associative object referencing the *client* and the *category*, including a date property, may be introduced.

- backtracking. The operations identified by the forward chaining of section 15.4.4 may result in the discovery of new object schemes containing them. The same occurs for the events identified by the backwards chaining of section 15.4.5.

As a result of this step, objects are identified, classified into object schemes and structural relationships among object schemes are properly specified in terms of composition, reference and inheritance links.

15.4.4 Identification of Operations

There are two ways of identifying operations. On each identified object scheme, the operations which may modify object states are introduced. For each identified event, the operations which are triggered are listed (forward chaining process).

15.4.5 Identification of Events

Three complementary approaches are possible.

- external events result of the real world analysis. They may be identified independently of any existing scheme. For example, in Figure 15.5, the discovery of the external events *order arrival, order cancellation* and *order delivery* results of the acquisition of the application domain knowledge.

- for each identified object, noteworthy state changes must be recognised as internal events. This is the case of the internal event *out of stock* in Figure 15.5.

- for each identified operation, their external or internal triggering events must be discovered and characterised (backwards chaining process).

15.5 Conclusion

An Object Oriented model and its associated methodological Guide-lines have been presented for the conceptual stage of the development of an Object Oriented database application. New features are added to the Object Oriented conceptual modelling and Object Oriented database development. The most important are:

- the composition and referring concepts, which allow us to differentiate two kinds of interrelations between objects and,

- the event concept which specifies the behavioural dependencies between objects.

Some important characteristics of the conceptual process, which have not been presented here, will, nevertheless, be taken into consideration. They are, principally, the specification reuse mechanism, the tracing mechanism to link up conceptual analysis and design concepts, the real world model (to define the notion of actor and its relationship with event) and an abstraction mechanism able to support the definition of objects at different level of details.

References

[1]   F. Bancilhon, 'Object Oriented Database Systems', *7th Symposium on Principles of Database Systems*, Austin, March 1988; J. Banerjee, H.T. Chou, J.F. Gaza, W. Kim, D. Woelk, N. Ballou, H.J. Kim, *Data Model Issues for Object Oriented Applications*, ACM TOIS, Vol 5, Nb1, 1987; G. Copeland, D. Maier, *Making Smalltalk a Database System*, ACM SIGMOD International Conference on Management of Data, 1984; D. Maier, J. Stein, A. Otis, A. Purdy, *Development of an Object Oriented DBMS*, ACM OOPSOLA International Conference, 1986; M. Stonebraker, L. Rowe, *The Design of POSTGRES*, ACM SIGMOD International Conference on Management of Data, 1986.

[2]   C. Cauvet, C. Rolland, C. Proix, 'A Design Methodology for Object Oriented Database', Proceedings of the International Conference on Management of Data, Hyderabad, India, 1989.

[3]   G.M. Nijssen, T.A. Halpin, *Conceptual Schema and Relational Database Design*, Prentice-Hall, 1989; G. Verheijen, J. Van Bekkum, *An Information Analysis Method*, IFIP TC8 International Conference on Comparative Review of Information Systems Methodologies, North Holland, 1982.

[4]   D.W. Shipman, *The Functional Data Model and the Data Language DAPLEX*, ACM TODS, Vol.6, Nb1, 1981.

[5]   C. Rolland, C. Richard, *The Remora Methodology for Information Systems Design and Management*, IFIP TC8 International Conference on Comparative Review of Information Systems Design Methodologies, North Holland, 1982; M.R. Gustafsson, T. Karlsson, J. Bubenko, *A Declarative Approach to Conceptual Information Modelling*, IFIP TC8 International Conference on Comparative Review of Information Systems Design Methodologies, North Holland, 1982.

[6]   J.M. Smith, D.C.P. Smith, *Database Abstractions: Aggregation and Generalisation*, ACM TODS, June 1977.

[7]   F. Bancilhon, 'Object Oriented Database Systems', *7th Symposium on Principles of Database Systems*, Austin, March 1988.

[8]   A. Sernadas *et al*, 'The Basic Building Block of Information Systems', *Information Systems Concept*, North Holland, Namur, 1989.

[9]   B. Meyer, *Object Oriented Software Construction*, Prentice-Hall International, Hemel Hempstead, 1988.

[10]   J.F. Costa, A. Sernadas, C. Sernadas, *OBL User's Manual*, Instituto, Superio Técnico, Lisbon, May 1989.

[11]   C. Rolland, O. Foucault, G. Benci, *Conception de systèmes d'information: la méthode REMORA*, Eyrolles, 1987; C. Cauvet, C. Rolland, C. Proix, 'A Design Methodology for Object Oriented Database', Proceedings of the International Conference on Management of Data, Hyderabad, India, 1989.

[12]   Edward Sciore, 'Object Specialisation', *ACM Transactions on Information Systems*, Vol.7, No.2, April 1989.

[13]   M.E.S. Loomis, A.V. Shah, J.E. Rumbaugh, *An Object Modelling Technique for Conceptual Design*, European Conference on Object Oriented Programming, Paris, June 1987.

[14]   J, Brunet, C. Cauvet, L. Lasoudris, 'Why Using Events in a High-Level Specification', *9th International Conference of Entity-Relationship Approach*, Lausanne, October 1990.

[15]   R. Elmasri *et al*, *Semantics of temporal data in an extended ER model*, 9th International Conference of Entity-Relationship Approach, Lausanne, October 1990.

[16]   A. Tsalgatidou, P. Loucopoulos, *An Object Oriented Rule-based Approach to the Dynamic Modelling of Information Systems*, International Working Conference on Dynamic Modelling of Information Systems, Noordwijkerhout, The Netherlands, April 1990.

[17]   G. Kappel, M. Schrefl, *Using an Object Oriented Diagram Technique for the Design of Information Systems,* International Working Conference on Dynamic Modelling of Information System, Noordwijkerhout, The Netherlands, April 1990.

BCS Data Management Specialist Group

The Data Management Specialist Group has regular meetings throughout the country, organises conferences and has a number of working parties. (SSADM, Data Administration and OODM). Membership is open to BCS and non-BCS members.

A comprehensive programme of regular meetings is arranged throughout the year. These regular meetings are a forum where data management personnel can discuss common interests and problems, topical aspects of relevance, including data analysis, database design, data dictionaries, CASE products, information resource planning and management. London meetings are held usually on Wednesday afternoons. In the North West, meetings are held in the evenings, usually at Manchester Polytechnic; there are similar regular meetings in Glasgow and Edinburgh and the South West branch of the DMSG organises meetings in Bristol. All members of the DMSG receive a quarterly newsletter, *Data Management Bulletin*, free of charge. This contains articles contributed by members and full details of DMSG meetings throughout the country.

The DMSG annual national conference BCS DATA MANAGEMENT YY is the year's focal point for members. The emphasis at these conferences is on practical and relevant Data Management problems within the business DP environment.

If you would like to know more about the DMSG, please contact the BCS Specialist Group Liaison Executive at The British Computer Society, PO Box 1454, Station Road, Swindon, SN1 1TG, England, telephone 0793 480269.

T - #0044 - 230425 - C0 - 297/210/6 [8] - CB - 9781138339347 - Gloss Lamination